STEPHANIE CALMAN

Confessions of a
Bad Mother
THE
TEENAGE
YEARS

PICADOR

First published 2019 by Picador

This paperback edition first published 2020 by Picador
an imprint of Pan Macmillan
The Smithson, 6 Briset Street, London EC1M 5NR
Associated companies throughout the world
www.panmacmillan.com

ISBN 978-1-5098-8213-7

9 8 7 6 5 4 3 2 1

A CIP catalogue record for this book is available from the British Library.

Typeset by Palimpsest Book Production Limited, Falkirk, Stirlingshire
Printed and bound by CPI Group (UK) Ltd, Croydon, CR0 4YY

Visit **www.picador.com** to read more about all our books
and to buy them. You will also find features, author interviews and
news of any author events, and you can sign up for e-newsletters
so that you're always first to hear about our new releases.

To Katarina

There *was* a Third Parent, Lawrence:
it just wasn't you.

Contents

Prologue

My daughter Lydia and I are in the formal wear department of BHS, buying her a dress.

My husband Peter's sister has found the last available sane heterosexual man in London and is getting married again. It's going to be a small event – no bridesmaids or best man or anything – but we're all going to dress properly. Peter's wearing a suit, and Lawrence has been given one by an older boy up the road. I've got a beautiful raspberry-coloured skirt from Reiss. So that just leaves Lydia. And BHS is *the* place for affordable wedding gear. Lydia isn't actually mad keen on dresses, but this is a wedding. You dress up. Right?

I immediately spot a dress in a lovely plum colour; you could cut out the label and say it's Monsoon.

'Isn't that lovely?'

Silence.

'Lydia, that's definitely one to try on.'

'No!'

'Just try it on.'

'NO!'

'For God's sake! Just choose *that one*!'

'*NO!!*'

Coming from a very minimal family, I've been starved of weddings – though not of divorces – and am very much looking forward to this one. In fact, the shortage of family weddings was a reason I decided to have one myself, which raised the number in my life up till then to two. And I'm damned if the issue of that happy union is going to fuck up number three. But she is mutinous.

'If you don't choose that dress I'm going to go home without you.'

Not really an option, but these are desperate times.

'I'm going to go home without *YOU*!'

We go on like this for what is probably only a few minutes – but feels like hours – until she grudgingly settles on a mid-length mauve number. It's not quite as classy as the plum but perfectly fine, with a little matching flower on the bodice and a bolero of embroidered net. Mission accomplished.

But we walk to the tube station in silence. We have the dress, yet there's no sense of achievement, or even relief – just a dull numbness. I'm like the Soviet Air Defence officer in the 1980s who saved the world when the 'Incoming Missile' signal lit up, by not pressing the red button. I get no parade, no outward sign of anything having been achieved. I'm just: not dead.

This overreaction to choosing *clothes*, for a *wedding* – which is meant to be A HAPPY OCCASION, FOR FUCK'S SAKE – has thrown me right off balance. When we get home I make some tea, but I feel utterly demoralized. Is it possible that our child has reached that stage which I know is coming, but is a good few years off? Not yet – surely it can't be!

She seems to be in the early stages of adolescence. And she is seven.

Ages 7 & 8: The Sticking Point

The summer holidays arrive and we go to the coast. The kids and I are walking alongside the low beach wall, and from nowhere, like a squall, a row starts up. Lawrence has somehow got a stick, and Lydia wants it.

'For God's sake,' I say, 'just get another stick.'

But no: they must both have *that* stick.

He gets up onto the wall, and she follows. He holds the stick out of her reach; she goes after it. They end up fighting each other along the narrow concrete ledge, like Errol Flynn and Basil Rathbone in *The Adventures of Robin Hood* (1938) but with more whining.

Then they both fall off.

You wouldn't believe a seven- and an eight-year-old could make that much noise. People driving past slow down to look, and a nearby builder briefly puts down his drill.

After a whole morning trying to entertain them, I have totally *had* it.

'STOP BLOODY FIGHTING! WHY WERE YOU

FIGHTING? NO WONDER YOU FELL OFF THE BLOODY WALL! WHAT D'YOU *EXPECT*?!'

'We-he-he werehhhhnt fi-hi-hi-ghting,' Lydia gasps between sobs, while Lawrence just lies on the ground, screaming.

I pick them up, look for injuries – can see none – fish around in the linty pockets of my non-attractive seaside coat, and find a chocolate-covered mint, slightly bent. And because I'm a parent, not a laboratory rat – and therefore don't learn from experience – I bring out the one mint before making sure there's a second.

There isn't a second.

And so they continue crying all the way to the sweet shop, where I buy them a tube of Smarties each because, whatever happens in life sugar will always be there for them, and take nothing in return but their health.

As a parent, I assume they fight in order just to ruin my day. However, David Attenborough says that young animals such as lion cubs attack each other as practice, for when they'll have to struggle for survival against predators. So it apparently has a purpose apart from to drive me off my head.

Not that I get this at the time.

And whether I take them to A&E, spend the rest of the day giving them treats or merely shout at them and cruelly force them to share a single bent mint will ultimately make no difference. They are developing in the way they need to. But, as I say, I don't know this yet. And if I did, it probably wouldn't help.

Mentally wrung out, I march them back and hand them over to Peter.

'I thought we were going to take turns,' he says.

'We have. I have. Your turn now.'

Still, tomorrow is another day.

Unfortunately.

Again they're fidgety and bored, so we get in the car to go down the coast a bit for a change of scene. They say the next town but one is lovely.

Maybe it's like the next-door queue in the supermarket or other people's marriages: better because you're never in it. Whatever it's like, it can't be worse than France last summer, when we drove for an hour to a chateau with a 'play area' which was literally a slide on a square of boiling-hot gravel. But, setting off for *anywhere* with children and any kind of expectations is probably an exercise in futility; most kids, most of the time, just want to play undisturbed with their building blocks or cars, or at a push some wet sand, and you generally don't need to go anywhere – apart from to those hangars of sensory assault by primary colours known as soft play centres, which they absolutely LOVE, and which for some reason I almost never go to without a raging hangover, or maybe I just acquire one while I'm there without even getting to be drunk first.

We leave late, and Lawrence is already getting low blood sugar. He and I have that sort of metabolism where we have to eat six times a day, and Lydia and Peter have the other kind. Where Lawrence's typical breakfast is bacon, eggs, toast and sausages, Lydia has half a mango and Peter just an apple because he ate in September.

Then, just as I realize Lawrence really has to eat soon – no, *now* – because he is getting psychopathic, we hit the main road, and a traffic jam. The other seaside town is only forty minutes away, but it's already taken us half an hour and we've only gone a mile up the road.

'Right, we have to find food! It's nearly lunchtime,' I say, resenting the fact that I'm always the one to have to point it out, and annoyed with myself because the only thing in my bag is a chocolate wafer which is technically Lydia's, because Lawrence had his yesterday. And anyway it's completely the wrong thing. Lydia agrees to share it, but it only restores Lawrence's sugar levels for about four seconds before he's writhing in agony on the back seat.

We turn off the main road and go another way.

'This is taking *ages*,' says Lydia.

'Who wanted to go to the seaside anyway?' says Lawrence.

'I did – so we wouldn't be cooped up in the house, getting on each other's nerves!'

'Well, it was a stupid idea.'

'I want to go home.'

Peter says, 'Come on, it'll be lovely! We're nearly there.'

'There's a shop,' I say. 'Let's get something there.'

But he drives past.

'It's almost lunchtime. I thought you said we were going for lunch.'

'I meant, to get something to keep him going. He *can't last*. Don't you understand?'

Then I spot a sweet little thatched tea room up ahead.

'That looks perfect. There – no – what are you doing?'

'Going to the *sea*,' he says through gritted teeth. 'Isn't that what you *wanted*?'

He keeps on going, past the tea room, to the end of the road, where it almost reaches the sea but ends in one of those compulsory car parks like at the Needles in the Isle of Wight, so you can't even get out and have a glimpse without paying £3. We can't see the sea at all. No wonder these places get vandalized. I feel quite strongly like getting out and smashing up a bus shelter myself.

'Surely,' I say, in my supposedly-patient-but-actually-quite-angry voice, 'we should have lunch, because everyone is *hungry* – except you of course – *then* come back here when we've eaten.'

'You wanted to look at the sea, so that's what we're doing. *All right?*'

'Why can't we just go *home*?' says Lawrence, using his last molecule of blood glucose to grimace horribly.

'Right, there's a pub,' Peter says. It has a sign outside advertising *Two Meals for the Price of One!* and karaoke.

'Don't be ridiculous,' I say. 'What was wrong with that tea room you drove past for some bizarre reason? You're always saying you don't want them eating junk food. Well, that's exactly what you'll get in there!'

'Right!'

He's now in his Basil Fawlty persona. He pulls out again, speeds up and just as I say:

'There's a speed camera!' I see a flash.

'Happy now?'

'Why the hell didn't you SLOW DOWN?'

Snorting at each other like bulls, we pull up outside

the tea room, hoping to God it's open. It is. A friendly-looking man waves us in, and then disappears into the kitchen, to be replaced by a sullen woman in a stained top. We go through a door and the sweet little thatched cottage turns into a freezing empty barn with an actual layer of dust on the table. We sit down and feel our bones contracting in shock.

'My God, it's colder in here than outside,' says Lawrence.

We huddle together in our seats.

'Could we have some menus?' I ask the woman.

'Yes, I'm just coming,' she replies, with an almost audible 'tch'.

'And could you possibly put the fire on?'

There is a coal-effect gas fire, concealed behind a screen.

'I will – in a minute!'

She switches on the fire, carefully keeping the screen in place to make sure none of the heat seeps out.

We open the menus. Not only is there no sign of the cream teas or snack meals listed outside on the jolly-looking blackboard, everything is absurdly expensive.

'Good choice,' says Peter. 'Thank God we didn't go to the place with two meals for the price of one.'

The main courses are at London prices. And even the 'Light Lunches' start at £9. We're not even in a town; we're in the middle of nowhere, for heaven's sake.

'Soup,' I say. 'They have soup!'

It's vegetable. By some miracle, both the children agree to have it, with a tomato and mozzarella salad for Lawrence as a chaser. Still, I'm envisaging the row when Lydia discovers a molecule of parsley and refuses to touch a drop.

A breakthrough: warm, crusty rolls arrive, which we swallow almost before they hit the plates. The soup is delicious. I contemplate ordering another round, but at £4.50 for about a cupful it's not really on.

'What's for pudding?' asks Lawrence.

'Er, we'll have that somewhere else,' Peter and I say simultaneously, the only thing we agree on being our desire to get away.

'Everything all right for you?' growls the woman.

'Lovely, thank you!'

We jump into the car and drive to Chichester. The sea is not mentioned again, and deploying only the minimum of communication we get out and have a round of hot chocolates in a Maison Blanc. The children also have a giant marshmallow each. While they sip their chocolates Peter and I read the papers in silence, waiting for the marriage to thaw out.

In a fleeting burst of maturity, I pay the exorbitant bill without letting him see it and restore some sensation of control.

As we're leaving, Lydia says:

'Mummy, if you do get a divorce, bagsy I live with you.'

And on that heart-warming note, we head home.

I've been assuming that it was just being on holiday that put everyone in a shit mood and that when they get back to their toys and their friends and their routine, the children will revert to their usual charming selves. The episode with Lydia in BHS was surely a one-off that will recede with time.

But then something else happens that really rattles me.

Lawrence starts answering back, throwing polite requests and totally normal questions back in my face, and generally not being very pleasant.

One evening, out of the blue, this happens:

'Lawrence,' I say, 'could you hang your blazer up?'

And he says:

'Why? You're nearest.'

Then, after supper, as he's sliding off to the TV, I ask:

'Could you please put your plate by the sink?'

And get in return:

'Why should I? You put it there.'

I've not even asked him to wash up. What the hell is happening here? Who is this horrible child?

'Excuse me?' I say. 'I put it there because I *just made and served your bloody dinner!* PUT YOUR PLATE UP *NOW!*'

When he's gone to bed I say to Peter:

'What the fuck's going *on*?'

'Oh, I'm sure it'll blow over.'

'Well, thanks for your input.'

He does come up with one useful idea though.

At bedtime, Lawrence has been saying he's not tired – as kids do – and Peter says:

'Why don't we try letting him read till a bit later?'

'OK. And he can turn his own light off.'

It seems a tiny thing, but it does the trick. Lawrence goes to bed more readily and his manners improve.

So, if we've just proved the equation *rudeness + more freedom = nicer behaviour*, then it's Good News: we've found a strategy. Less Good News: this is absolutely the definition of adolescence, which was meant to be at least four years away.

'But!' says Peter, 'we've found a strategy.'

'And – but – *BUT*' I say, 'if this is what I think it is, we're looking at ten more years.'

Aristotle said: 'Give me a child until he is seven, and I will give you the man' – or, to be more accurate, the quite annoying young adult. So maybe adolescence really does begin then; it's just taken us 2,300 years to notice.

Then I come across something a friend told me years ago: that the end of childhood comes at the age of seven. Up until then, you believe a golden pony really could come cantering round the corner, and after that age, you know it won't. What they should have added was: after that you begin to shout at your parents for no reason. And *we're* the ones still waiting for that golden pony.

We cling to the belief that our children are sweet, innocent creatures. We know that *one day* they will wake up horribly changed, a mutant snarling and spitting beast, but believe that day is comfortably far off.

So, instead of paying attention to the signs, which start long before that, we believe in a kind of reverse creation myth: after eleven or twelve years of 'normality' comes a catastrophe like the meteor that destroyed the dinosaurs – and our hitherto nice children metamorphose into Teenagers.

And we're not only unprepared but amazed, indignant even, that this outrage should be perpetrated on *us*. We've fed and clothed them, woken up in the night, taken them to soft play centres, sung 'The Wheels on the Bus' and suffered for them in all sorts of ways. And now we're being punished!

They've been saying for years that 'puberty starts earlier and earlier these days'. But that's not it at all. In fact, now, after twenty years, looking at the whole picture, I think this – the striving for autonomy, the battling over trivia – *is* normality. And coming out the other side of it – if we make it that far – is the transformation.

To return, then, to the summer holidays of 2006, and the endless quest for something to do.

It is the time of the annual Hand-Wringing Festival, when simple newspaper folk publish surveys bemoaning the Loss of Proper Childhoods, due to the demise of traditional games. Children don't play board games or hopscotch any more; tree climbing and den building have died out, and we're all going to hell in an Xbox.

Actually, they may have a point.

First it was *Club Penguin*. Then *Animal Crossing*. Now they're fighting fire and ice monsters, who all have different powers, with warriors who each have certain attributes and so on – though all the various creatures seem to do when attacked is jump into the air and back down again.

This strikes me as supremely unexciting, but Lawrence and Lydia are both hooked. Geomag, Sylvanians, Her Little Ponies – all the old favourites lie abandoned on the floor. Negotiating the number of hours allowed on it starts before breakfast. When friends come to play, their eyes light up and they too gather round the screen.

'What's the point of having friends to play if you don't *play*?' I say.

'We *are* playing. We're playing *Adventure Quest*!'

Is that it? Is their childhood over already?

At pick-up time, the school playground usually rings to the squeals of Lydia and her classmates as they play Bulldog, running past whoever's It to touch the playground wall. Will it now fall silent? At home I want to fight my way through piles of cushions to the upturned sofa, the children's presence given away by the trail of cheese-triangle wrappers leading to the blanket-covered entrance of their den, where only last month a visiting Barbie lay under a tent of fleece having a baby, directed by the most brutally unsympathetic midwives.

'Push! That's it! Right, back to work.'

17

Stephanie Calman

And I almost tear up with nostalgia when I delve under the stairs looking for the picnic blanket and find Lawrence's longbow.

On our most recent visit to my mum's, in a village which boasts a real, live Village Green, he made a bow out of a curved stick and a length of string. It looked completely harmless but was in fact able to fire the lethally sharp twigs he'd whittled clear across the green, narrowly missing the heads of two mesmerized small boys who'd come out to watch. One landed in a neighbour's garden, just as her dog stopped barking.

Meanwhile, Lydia sat on the grass with another neighbour's kids, collecting leaves and weaving them into little bowers while my mother and I watched them in a trance of parental – and grandparental – ecstasy. They played out there right up to suppertime, pausing only to come in and moan at us for letting them miss *The Simpsons*.

I am *so* grief-stricken for their younger selves I even start to miss Ludo, Snakes and Ladders and Monopoly: really quite boring games – and in the case of Monopoly potentially endless as well, culminating, every time, in Lawrence getting Park Lane and Mayfair and his father and me each owing him £50,000 in rent and pleading with him and Lydia to please, *please* go and watch some TV.

After four weeks of *Adventure Quest* I pull myself together and try to think what Mary Poppins would do.

I harangue them about the enfeeblement of their constitutions until they agree to get dressed and leave the house – to walk, rollerblade, stand outside for half an hour picking their noses – anything that involves actual bodily contact with fresh air. Or that gets me to shut up. We walk briskly round the park, and gradually the air clears.

When we come back in I steer them firmly past the computer and towards the stairs.

'You can do anything you like,' I say, 'apart from go on the computer.'

I issue Peter my Standard Warning Look – *Do Not Give Way On This Or I Will Hurt You* – and steel myself. I can stand it if they burst into tears; I don't even care any more if they hate me; I just wish they would go back to being our adorable children who used to make dens. But they don't burst into tears and they don't say they hate me. And after about ten seconds, Lawrence says,

'Can we make a den?'

When I come back an hour later they're sitting on the floor in his room under two chairs and a duvet, and Lydia is reading to him from a book of stories I bought at a jumble sale for 10p.

So my message to parents – and the compilers of surveys – is this: today, *Adventure Quest*; tomorrow, two chairs and a duvet. But don't go and spoil their fun with your mealy-mouthed, modern caution. As Lawrence said when he made the bow and I warned him not to shoot anyone in the eye:

'Stop complaining. You wanted us to play outside, didn't you?'

Guerrillas in the Mist

Peter's from Sheffield, on the edge of the Peak District National Park. He grew up with some of Britain's most beautiful landscape at the end of his road, while my view was of a pub and its customers coming out to pee in the neighbouring doorways, including ours. And whereas I grew closer to my father at the National Film Theatre, he bonded with his on Kinder Scout: formative experiences we have carried with us, beyond their deaths and throughout our lives.

'I'm going to take Lawrence to climb Mount Snowdon,' he announces one day. 'It's a proper mountain. And, unlike the others, it's really picturesque. *And* you can do it in a day.'

He is only eight though.

'A tiny bit young?' I say.

'I used to go fell-walking with my father: it'll be great!'

'I thought you had to be dragged along because

you'd rather have been sitting in your room, playing with your cars.'

'Er, but I loved it when I got there and got into it. You just can't appreciate the character-building qualities of a long uphill walk in dense cloud.'

'Clearly. Well, have a wonderful time.'

It's an unspoken covenant of the marriage that I'm head of all things artsy-fartsy-crafty-wafty, while he's in charge of activities likely to result in falls from steep rocks.

When Peter's stepmother died and the Sheffield house had to be sold, we had a magical ten days there, which included a walk up the escarpment known as Stanage Edge, Derbyshire's answer to Uluru. And the children, who were five and six at the time, got up onto the rock plateau at the top and ran about.

And every time they neared the edge, I thought I was going to throw up or faint. So I did the only thing I could do that wouldn't provoke a row with Peter or spoil their fun; I turned round and forced myself to look the other way. My mother has on her wall the picture Lawrence drew of them as stick figures on what looks like a pile of huge boulders in mid-air. Which is pretty much as I remember it.

Peter plans the assault on the north face with military precision. He requisitions maps and over-trousers, prepares a rucksack of ham and cheese rolls to keep low blood sugar at bay, and plots the scenic route, the other side from the mountain railway.

The going is good and the ham rolls do their work, but as they near the summit, low cloud appears and engulfs them in wet mist.

And on the way down Peter takes a wrong turn.

And because the only way to reconnect with the right track is to go up – *then* down, he has to confess.

Team morale plummets.

Lawrence lies down in the wet heather, unable to go on.

'I just want to go home.'

But there is nothing Peter can do.

'I'm really sorry. I've made a mistake.'

And Lawrence accepts it.

Like Joe Simpson up the Andes with his smashed leg in *Touching the Void*, he pulls himself up and resumes the bid for base camp – a B&B at Betws-y-Coed.

They can see the ghostly shapes of other climbers in the mist, and tantalizingly, the sound of the mountain railway just a few metres away. But the summit is cloaked in cloud, obscuring the little terminus. And besides, he hasn't even admitted to Lawrence that there is a train, which is clearly audible.

Now its existence has been revealed, but even if

they *could* reach it, it would take them down the wrong side, six miles from where they've left the car. And anyway you can't get on if you haven't booked.

Because of his mistake, the only possible route left to them – that they can actually *see* – is one that gets progressively steeper. Eventually they are at a gap with a twenty-foot or so drop that Lawrence is too small to cross. Some of the ghostly shapes materialize beside them, and Peter hands Lawrence to another climber across the gap.

After what seems a long time, they end up at the car park, and ultimately a pub tikka masala and a Simpsons comic. So, at the tender age of eight, Lawrence learns the value of not losing your nerve when things go wrong, and has no urge to learn it again. At least not up a Welsh mountain in the mist.

And only when they're safely back home does Peter confess to me just *how* steep it was, and *how* sheer the drops.

'Jesus. I am so glad I didn't know that.'

'But what the experience really showed,' he says, 'is, when it came to a crisis, Lawrence's attitude was extremely positive.'

'Because it was that or stay there and die in the heather.'

'Well, that's putting a different spin on it.'

Spin's the word all right. Though I know Lawrence behaved well and am pleased, I don't want to let Peter get away with all this crap about how marvellous it was getting lost and taking my eight-year-old down a series of lethal drops when they couldn't bloody see.

'It was certainly a golden opportunity for him to learn his father isn't perfect.'

'Exactly! A key moment.'

How does he *do* that?

Still, if going up, then down, then up again, then down a mountain isn't a metaphor for growing up, I don't know what is.

'Well done, Lawrence,' I say. 'Were you scared?'

'Not really,' he says. 'Only when Daddy looked down and I saw his face.'

Then Peter takes Lydia. She nips up the 1,085 metres on just a bowl of Rice Krispies and a boiled egg, and at the summit, gazing across the perfectly clear sky towards Ireland, begins her passionate affair with the outdoors. Her after-treat is not a curry and a comic in a nice cosy pub, but a visit to the local stables for a pony ride.

For her, this is just the beginning.

At Lawrence's school Open Day there's a sign inviting visitors to have a go in a kayak. Her face lights up.

She borrows a swimming costume from somewhere and goes in.

'Hang on – when did she learn to dive?'

'No idea.'

The teacher says,

'Good! Right, now flip the kayak all the way over and back up again.'

And she does – just like that. When she springs up, she is soaking wet and elated.

The teacher is also the expedition leader on Lawrence's next school trip: canoeing on the river Wye. And she invites Lydia to join them on the spot.

The trip is intriguingly subtitled: 'An Introduction to Moving Water. Bring your own marshmallows.'

Lydia swings into action, and marks out five days in her diary: three days of camping and paddling preceded by two of packing. And before she's even left she passes a milestone of her own: her bag contains all the thick socks, fleeces, sleeping bags, hot chocolate sachets and pasta specified on the kit list, and no more than one cuddly toy.

As usual Peter scoops up all the credit. Whenever anyone asks, 'What're you doing at half-term?' he says:

'Well, the kids are kayaking down the River Wye. They take after my father, of course.'

And the image you have is of the solitary explorer, steadfastly paddling through deserted waters with just a tin cup and a bedroll, and a lone eagle wheeling overhead, as opposed to fully risk-assessed, safety-checked children smothered in lifejackets and helmets, in a group supervised by two completely trained adults with enough kit for an invasion.

Peter's strategy of claiming the credit for his long-departed father is clever because it appears not to favour him, but the former parent – who can't be smug because he's dead. Claiming credit for your children's achievements – while appearing not to – is now even more popular than skiing.

But he and I are also facing a step into the unknown.

This is the first time they've ever both been away at the same time, without either of us.

'We're off the leash,' he says. 'We can do literally *anything*.'

We wave them off in their minibus and drive to the South Downs, where we completely let ourselves go: poached eggs with extra toast and two coffees each, then a walk, then a two-hour lunch followed by slow browse round the bookshops of Lewes, topped off by a fabulous dinner and comatose slumber in a big fat B&B bed, all made by someone else.

At breakfast the next morning, he says:

'You do realize this is the future?'

'What, fabulous dinners and big fat beds all made by other people . . .?'

No, I know what he means.

'Just the two of us.'

Gulp.

I've only just got used to being *four*.

I used to think the future would wait its turn, not happen while you're still grappling with the present.

Then the expedition leader rings to tell us that Lawrence is not well.

'He's in his tent with a tummy upset.'

Peter puts his hand over the phone.

I assume he's going to say: *He's such a Calman.* But he looks quite concerned.

'What'll we do? Drive to Wales and get him, or . . .'

I consider the time it'll take from Sussex – at least five hours. And there's another tea room I want to try.

Down the line from the Wye Valley, Lawrence sounds very small yet not entirely desperate to come home.

'He's with the school – and Lydia. He's quite safe, and maybe he'll feel a bit humiliated if we take him away. I think we should leave him, but get an update later today.'

To my surprise, the person suggesting this is me.

By the evening we've heard nothing and as they're due home the next day we decide to relax.

'Maybe,' says Peter, 'your desire for a child-free weekend is simply stronger than your separation anxiety.'

'Well, I do love a tea room.'

Perhaps when the time comes for them to move out, this selfishness of mine will be an asset.

But maybe it's easier to be the 'strong' one if the other shows their anxiety first.

When we get back, the expedition leader sends us a letter congratulating Lydia on having completed two nine-mile runs in a kayak, 'seal launched' into the river down a chute, run some 'grade two rapids', built a fire and – the most mysterious process of all – put up and packed away her own tent.

'And,' says Lydia, 'the teacher brought along her dog!'

I tell my mother, a lifelong nature-lover and former youth hosteller. She is mystified.

'You and your sister were never at all interested in all that.'

'I know! Weird, isn't it?'

She loved the natural world and would almost certainly have carried on strolling about Scotland in shorts and thick socks had she not gone to London and met my father, for whom nature was seen ideally through a window over tea and hot buttered toast.

'And guess what? Jon and Lucy have invited her to something called Hippy Camp.' They're the parents of Milo, Lawrence's friend since the age of two.

'Is that its actual title?'

'It's near Totnes, so you never know. It's inspired by Rudolf Steiner.'

'Well, he was a bit of crank, letting children paint only in pastel colours and planting by the phases of the moon and so on. But – you know, pretty harmless.'

Unlike me, when she has an opinion about this kind of thing, it's backed up by having read the original text.

When Lydia hears that she's going to a soggy field in the West Country for a week of bushcraft, storytelling and making dreamcatchers, she's ecstatic. She's even fascinated by the prospect of alternative lavatory facilities.

'What are earth loos? Never mind! I can't wait!'

There's also a Healing Tent. Before I can compose my regretful refusal, Lucy texts:

You'd HATE it.

'She knows me better than you do,' I tell Peter, who actually suggests I join them. He sends me the highlights:

Bushcraft
Eurythmics in the Chi tent
Swordwork for the over-15s
Willow sculpture for adults
Talk on living buildings
Zipwire in the indigo village
Teepee time (for little ones)
Felt headbands for 7–12s
Labyrinth creation
Chi healing in the teen yurt.

Beads, tie-dye, sandals, Crocs n ponchos r the Look. Also, long grey hair n no bras. He adds: *Fantastic curries made by Jon on the fire* – the only part of it he knows I will look upon with envy.

Lydia is in her element – in *the* elements. After two days Lawrence gets a chest infection from the constant rain and damp and, after a failed attempt to dry out in a launderette in Totnes, is brought home early with suspected swine flu. When I take him to the GP, we're told to get out before he infects anyone, take Tamiflu and stay in for at least ten days. I ask my ex-nurse friend J what to do.

'Oh, if he *was* infectious it's too late to worry about it now.'

So we go to the library and take out a load of DVDs.

Meanwhile Lydia darts through the drizzle from horse care to weaving to archery, pausing only to wolf down a biodynamically grown falafel burger.

You can see the dominant characteristics as clearly as if their DNA was actually visible – like that moment in *The Matrix* when Neo learns that the girl in the red dress is only lines of code:

Grimsdale = skipping cheerfully through the rain whittling a willow wand; Calman = sitting in a warm, dry room watching *Family Guy*.

Pret à Shouter

Like Lawrence's pet stick insects, Lydia sheds her outer layers with impunity. When she's finished with something, or grows out of it, she simply sloughs it off. To find anything, you have to count through the layers till you get to the day she last wore it, and below that are things she hasn't worn for years. Dig all the way down and you may find babygros.

'That could be a TV show,' says Peter. 'A group of children have to perform various tasks, such as putting away their football kit or picking up their dirty clothes. Then each week the father sends one of them to their room, points at them and shouts: "You're Tired!"'

My father was actually quite like Alan Sugar when he lost his temper – scarier, actually, since what began as a growl would rise in pitch almost to a scream. And one of the worst battlegrounds, which led to absolutely massive rows, was what we were supposed to wear.

My mother didn't mind, and in any case she never took us anywhere formal. As I say, we had so little family that there were no weddings or anniversary parties – well, one during my entire childhood – so it never came up.

But then my father and stepmother came back from holiday married, and his new in-laws Had Standards. Before a visit to her parents, they would demand we brush our hair and put on dresses. And we would refuse. Christmas was a particular flashpoint.

'It's just this bloody ONCE!' Dad would shout. And my stepmother would complain that we were 'badly brought up'.

It just made no sense to us, putting on different clothes to eat lunch. Now, when I think of all the rules we *could* have mutinied over, it seems so trivial, a typical protest of the disenfranchised.

But now I'm on the receiving end, because Lydia's doing it as well!

Given that Peter and I are frankly much better parents than mine ever were, this is NOT BLOODY FAIR. And now we are coming up to a major test.

My friend Diane is getting married.

We've already been through the hell of buying Lydia a dress. In fact it's a year since Lydia and I had the row in BHS – that's how I know it's Peter's sister's first wedding anniversary. Or perhaps I should say first-second, since she's on number two. Second timers probably have a separate anniversary gift chart by now, where having been given a load of mostly pointless stuff the first time round, you start getting rid of it all: first anniversary, chuck out something made of paper; second: something cotton – the *decree nisi* perhaps, followed by your ex-mother-in-law's dreadful curtains.

Anyhow, my old friend Diane is getting married – for the first time, in a beautiful old building with a proper sit-down lunch and an entertainer for the children – and only a short drive from where we live. It will be literally stress free.

Peter gets Lawrence into the hand-me-down suit again. The trousers are still too long; height-wise he's a Calman and short for his age, so everything is. I quickly take them up, leaving a nice neat outline interrupted only by a big lump of folded fabric halfway down his calves. But he puts them on happily without a peep.

'He takes after me,' says Peter.

'Shut up. We're going to be late.'

I can't *stand* being late.

I turn my attention to Lydia, who's still in her pyjamas.

'OK, Lydsy, time to put on your lovely mauve dress.'

'I'm not wearing THAT!'

'What? You chose it!'

'I wanted the *other one*.'

Excuse me?

'You are *joking*.'

'I want to wear the circle top.'

Oh no.

No, no, no, NO.

This cannot be happening.

It's like a horror film where they've failed to lock the cellar door.

When we were away one weekend, I spotted a shop selling good second-hand clothes for kids, where I picked up, along with two T-shirts for £2 each, a rather groovy black top with pink and white circles on it: a nod towards Sixties pastiche, but with some naff drawstring ties at the hem. Thinking I had a good five years to cut those off, make it a bit more Austin Powers, maybe get her to team it with a mini skirt and white boots, I stuffed it into the back of her wardrobe. I did not hide it, bury it, or remove it to a safe place to be destroyed in a controlled explosion. So yes: Oh, Mea Culpa, goddess of motherhood, it is my bloody fault.

'It's way too big – and old – for you,' I told her, 'but you can grow into it.'

I then watched in horror as she got home, put it

on and has refused to be separated from it for the past four weeks. Quite often she sleeps in it, paired with *decorated tracksuit bottoms* passed on by some careless older girl. You know who you are.

'*Why* can't I wear it?' she says, as the clock ticks on and the wedding guests gather and sip their first glasses of champagne.

It hangs right off one shoulder, and – with her hair all straggly because she currently refuses to let me brush, clip *or* tie it – she looks like an unemployed lap dancer.

'You are absolutely *not wearing that top*.'

'FINE.'

Staring at me, her jaw set, she starts *putting on her jeans*.

I get no help from Peter, who is completely ready and downstairs with Lawrence, smugly reading a car magazine.

This kind of immovable pig-headedness can be an invaluable attribute – at times, in certain walks of life – for instance if you're Winston Churchill in 1940, trying to convince your fellow politicians not to make peace with a genocidal psychopath murdering his way across Europe. But coming from an eight-year-old, it is exhausting and debilitating.

I cannot go on.

I'm going to scream at her until she feels really fucking sorry, then hurl myself into the traffic.

I am At The End.

'Everything all right up there?' calls Peter.

I'm going to kill him as well.

But what's this? An impeccably timed text from our friend Federico, who is coming for dinner tomorrow with his Brazilian girlfriend.

See you at eight. We have news!

Taking a wild guess, could *he* be getting married too . . .?

O – M – G . . .

'Hey, Lydia! If you put on the mauve dress for Diane's wedding, now, this minute, so we're not incredibly, unforgivably late and she never speaks to me again – you can have a new one for Fed's. OK?'

'Really? Oh thank you, Mummy!'

She immediately puts it on and even *lets me brush her hair*.

Yet I feel not triumphant, merely worn out, and though she has put the bloody thing on, ineffective. I'm also in for at least another thirty quid on a second dress.

But the mauve garment is in position. The circle top has been stood down. And we can, finally, leave for the wedding.

The event is beautiful, and Diane's son Jack – who isn't yet ten – makes a moving speech that has every parent in the room thinking: *I bet my child couldn't do that*. Or maybe that's just me.

The following evening Federico comes over. He and Lucia are indeed engaged, and we're all invited!

And the wedding is this winter, in Brazil.

But by then, no doubt, we'll be facing challenges as yet unimagined.

Ages 8 & 9: The Brace Position

In my family, we had no strategies to deal with stress. Losing his temper was my father's default response to just about any provocation and so reflexive I assumed it was inevitable. Hungry? Got a parking fine? Getting divorced again? Why not lose your temper?! It was only years later I began to wonder how other people had discovered another way.

Lawrence has to have a brace. The orthodontist has identified a hereditary underbite on Peter's side, which may become a problem when his jaw stops growing, sometime after the age of sixteen. It could mean some quite scary surgery. But sixteen is seven years away, so far in the future we can't imagine it. And for the moment, luckily, all the brace has to do is redirect a single tooth that's growing outwards, as if trying to get away. But he's much younger than the usual age for these things, and it feels quite daunting.

Peter rings me from McDonald's, our traditional

venue for post-dentist treats, to say he can't eat, speak or swallow with it in.

'I don't know how we're going to do this,' he admits, in an unprecedented surrender to defeat.

But though Peter makes 'What a nightmare!' faces at me when they come in, Lawrence himself says nothing. In fact, he settles down calmly with a comic. As someone who at twelve dumped my prescription glasses with one eye blacked out – so my lazy-eye was never fixed – I am in awe. It looks horrendously uncomfortable.

'You are being so good,' I say. 'You can't eat or speak, and you're not even in a bad mood!'

And he takes the brace out and says:

'But Mummy: being in a bad mood doesn't *do* anything.'

Oh.

My.

God.

With this apparently casual remark our nine-year-old has reversed one of the core beliefs of my upbringing. Is this child in Year Four – not even at secondary school – more mature than my *dad*?

'Basically,' says Peter, 'most people are more mature than your dad.'

True.

'But he's nine: I can't believe it.'

Our child already understands that there's no point trying to blame anyone, because this temporary torture isn't being *inflicted* on him: it's for his benefit.

'It's OK,' he adds. 'Because I can take it out for meals. See?'

'Well done,' I say. 'I'm just so proud of you.'

'He takes after me,' says Peter. 'Now he can teach you how to be more positive as well.'

'Thank you: that *is* kind.'

Lawrence has lost ten teeth so far; Lydia has her eighth wobbler on the go. This week he brought home a certificate that says his handwriting is now neat enough to be done in ink. And they've both been on their own to the shop at the end of the road. Each stage of development is a great achievement!

I wonder what the next one will be?

Whenever it's my turn to walk Lawrence to school, we talk pretty much the whole twenty-five minutes from our front door to theirs. Today he tells me about his gang.

'It's called the Black Tigers. Or we might change it to the Black Panthers.'

'Actually,' I say, 'I'd stick to Tigers.'

'Why?'

'We-ell . . .'

I feel I had better nip this in the bud. Cultural Appropriation isn't yet a Thing, but there may be those who take exception to a clutch of fresh-faced white kids naming themselves after the militant yet socially ambitious black activists of the 1960s.

'Once upon a time in America' – I actually do say this – 'the white people were very cruel and unfair to the black people – well it's not that great now, but anyway. Some brave black men – and I think some women – got together and . . .'

He stops, to push the toe of his newly polished shoe into a puddle. Poor kid; he only wants to know the difference between a tiger and a panther – possibly not even that – and I'm giving him the history of the civil rights movement as it might be explained on CBBC. I pause. To my relief, he seems not to notice. Let's just hope the junior Black Panthers go the way of *Candida*, the 1970s women's magazine that was going to name itself after the medical term for thrush.

'We all control different things. I control the wind.'

I refrain from asking if this is in tribute to his prodigious bouts of farting.

'And do the others control fire and water and so on?'

'Yes!'

He seems to have it covered. I back off.

Then as we get near the school gate, he stops and turns round.

'It's OK. You can go now.'

Eh?

But I always walk him to the door.

'Oh. Well, OK. Are you sure?'

'I am *nine*.'

He looks at me resolutely.

'Yes. Of course. Well, bye!'

I walk back, feeling the loose end of an incomplete manoeuvre, as if I've left the car half out of a parking space or put on only one shoe.

That night I come into Lydia's room to see if she's persisting with *Black Beauty* as I'm hoping, or has reverted to the incredibly dull fairy books she's currently addicted to, a few lines of which make you long to be rescued by a brain haemorrhage. I peer over the bed and what is she reading? *Easy Living*. I know girls like to read a few years above their age; at sixteen we bought *Cosmopolitan*. But this is ridiculous.

'Hi, Mummy. Nice jackets, don't you think?'

Whoa!

She's *eight*.

She's also been experimenting with mascara. I say

'experimenting', but while the popular perception of little girls with make-up on is always of smeared lipstick and bright red circles of rouge like clowns in drag, she appeared in front of me the other day with her lashes just a little darker, and her lips subtly pink. It's unsettling.

I go down and tell Peter that ingesting this magazine makes our daughter prematurely susceptible to the pernicious influence of mass media and their unachievable standards for women, and that if *I'm* concerned, the least *he* can do is be worried as well.

'At least she's reading,' he says, without looking up. 'That's a good thing, right?'

Mm, passive-aggressive: my favourite!

No, he's right.

Non-school, fun reading is vital if they're to survive the unimaginative British education system and not end up hating books forever. And if it happens to contain headlines like 'Is that Freckle Cancer?' then so be it. The school reading scheme is *so* deadly it makes my reading book at this age, *The Pancake*, seem a classic of suspense.

On the other hand, each year – no, each *week* pretty much – they not only learn something, but advance in far more important ways which are of vital significance to *them*, some of which we parents don't even notice.

So when Lydia says she can't move up to Year Three in September we don't realize she's devastated.

'What? Why?'

'Because I haven't finished writing out the instructions for How to Use a Magnifying Glass!'

'What? Don't be ridiculous.'

Then I remember when the head of my primary school said that if I didn't finish *New Maths One*, I wouldn't get into secondary school. I didn't know I already had a place. My mother simply brushed my fears aside. But I only stopped worrying when I got to the new school and discovered that no one else had finished *New Maths One* either. In fact, most of them had never even heard of it.

And now here I am, doing exactly what my mother did: failing to sympathize, and invalidating the child's version of events so they feel even more helpless and wretched.

I hate myself.

Nonetheless, it does sound a bit unlikely.

'Daddy and I have been to the Moving Up Evening, and your name is definitely there. We saw it, honestly.'

'NO I CAN'T!' she cries. 'They won't let me!!'

She bangs her head onto her folded arms. Her despondency is total – though not enough to make her actually do the task.

This is the moment where I should remember my irrational headmistress, and my own despair, and talk to the school. But I'm a parent now and have moved up to the place where I cannot fully see or hear her pain.

And, in a sense, Lydia doesn't need the instructions for How to Use a Magnifying Glass, because that's the thing about being small: everything is already much bigger.

The summer holiday is already a vast unbroken plain of time stretching into infinity. It's going to be hard enough without this hanging over us.

'Don't worry,' says Peter. 'She'll have forgotten about it by the end of the week.'

Sure enough, he is right.

I will put it out of my mind but remain at the worry stop, for there is always another one on the way.

On a main road two streets from where we live, a man with ginger hair has attempted to abduct three eleven-year-olds on their way home from school, Or, to be precise, he has tried to pick up one of them and run off with her, but been fought off by her and the other two.

So both good news there, and bad.

Bad: it's not the first time this has happened in

our area. Good: thanks to the courage of the children involved, he failed and was arrested not long afterwards at the station, waiting for his getaway train:

'Any distinctive characteristics?'

'Apart from the bright orange hair . . .?'

And an IQ that inspired him to put his escape in the hands of Southern Rail.

Being one of the nearest, Lydia's school writes to the parents advising all children to stay inside the playground until they're collected, something they do already. In fact, because the outside space at the front is so small, they never come out until their parent is identified and matched up with them.

So I write back, pointing out that their advice doesn't address the issue of walking home, i.e. *The* Issue. But I do wonder afterwards if they're only really concerned with their end of it. Lydia will *want* to walk by herself well before Year Six. We live very close after all. And saying, 'Stay in' or 'Don't go anywhere alone' is not the solution.

I also tell the school I've explained to both children what they should do if this happens to them.

'So,' I say, 'you're walking back from school or whatever . . .'

'But you and Daddy take us,' says Lydia.

'Yes, I know, but in future. Or if you're going to

the shop. A guy comes up behind you, or leans out of a car. What do you do?'

'Go into a shop?'

'Good! Even before that? If he's trying to grab you, make as loud a noise as you can, and attack him back.'

Some may think this unrealistic for an eight- and a nine-year-old, but I don't want to instil the idea that they're powerless. A few years back, I saw a policeman on *Oprah* telling women that 'The last thing they expect is for you to fight back,' and when asked, 'But what if he threatens to kill me?' he said that most criminals are also liars, and murder 'almost never happens' as a result.

So, with those words of reassurance in mind, I repeat:

'Kick him – in the balls if you can manage it. Or scratch – scratching is good, because then you can get some DNA under your nails and they've got a better chance of catching him. Shout or scream, scratch, run. Got it?'

I watch their faces for signs of anxiety. I want them to absorb the advice, but not dwell on the danger. However they don't look anxious – they look bored.

'Shout, scratch, run,' says Lawrence. 'Can we go now?'

We will have this conversation again.

Conflict Resolution

Are you ever too young to learn conflict resolution?

Lydia's had an argument with her friend Poppy, who has knocked over her jewellery stand, sending about twenty sets of beads onto the floor. Now the two of them are in separate rooms, not speaking.

I go in and tell her:

'Stop this at once. She's your guest!'

'I don't care!'

'Is any of the stuff broken?'

'No.'

'Well then!'

It's not physically possible to get in and out of the area without stepping on something or knocking something over. I know, because the central heating timer is in her cupboard, and every autumn, while other people are raking fallen leaves, I have to clear a path through the dolls, bags, horses, diaries and half-used bead sets to reach the 'On' switch. And even then, as I pivot on one tiptoe to come back again, I usually emerge with a My Little Cocktail Glass or Sylvanian coatstand stuck to my foot.

'Go and say sorry. *Now.*'

'NO!'

Like parents who want their children to learn the piano because they didn't, I want her to learn conflict resolution even more because I have no skills in this area myself. I grew up with one passive-aggressive parent and one aggressive-aggressive one. My father blew up a lot, but my mother provoked him. And as they were useless at compromise, rows generally ended when he broke something and stormed out. So what I've learned from that is to boil silently then explode: the worst of both worlds. Plus when the children fight, I reward their bad behaviour by giving them lots of the Wrong Attention. And when I try to apply sanctions, I get *that* wrong as well. Not long ago I told them:

'If you carry on arguing you won't get any pocket money today.'

And Lawrence said,

'Pocket money day's on Friday.'

'Oh, I thought today was Friday.'

And he sighed before turning back to his comic.

'At least try to threaten us properly.'

But he and Lydia were soon chatting away again, like a warring couple brought together by their shared contempt for a useless relationship counsellor. So my strategy worked, in a way.

Suddenly I realize Poppy's mother is due any minute to collect her, so I rush back in and persuade the girls to watch television – anything to break the stalemate before the other parent arrives. Though not a recognized mediation technique, it works, and I see them do their joke air-kisses as they say goodbye. The next day we get comics, and Lydia chooses a Robin Hood one. Inside there are free postcards of the characters in the TV series, and she writes one to Poppy:

> *Dear Poppy,*
> *Let's never ever have another argument.*
> *Love Lydia xxx*

Is that it? Is what I've been missing all these years something that simple: a six-word declaration of peace that brings the dispute to an end without blame on either side. Is it generational? Or is everyone better at this than me?

That she's chosen the Sheriff of Nottingham card rather than Robin or Marian is quite amusing, though; she loves her friend, but not quite enough to give away her favourite ones. At least I assume it's that, rather than a subliminal endorsement of the medieval despot's own style of conflict resolution, namely imprisonment, extortion, crushing small birds in cages and death by hanging.

'Do you fall out with your friends?' I ask Lawrence the next day.

'All the time.'

But he can't say how things are resolved: lessons start again, or the subject is changed, and the problem goes away. Once, waiting in the lunch queue, he was punched in the head by another boy. When the school rang to tell me, I was beside myself.

'That's that same boy who picked on him before!' I said. 'You'd better tell me you're getting his parents in.'

'Well, there was probably something on both sides.'

Oh, right. Remember the UN in former Yugoslavia? I rest my case.

'Well!' I tell Lawrence firmly. 'I'll be making sure they deal with it, you can be sure of that.'

But instead of falling gratefully into my arms with a 'Thank you Mummy!' he said,

'Oh, it's all fine now.'

'What? That awful boy who punched you?'

'I'm saying: don't do anything.'

He gave me a 'duh' look and went back to his homework.

I never had quarrels with my friends. There was one who was very changeable – a good laugh one day, in a huge sulk the next. But I never dealt with it. I can't have arguments with people because I don't know how to continue beyond them. If there's a problem I have no strategy except to run away. There's no question: at eight and nine the children are already far more adept at these things than I was – or probably ever will be.

'What?' says Peter. 'You argue with *me*.'

'That's different.'

I argue with him because we live in the same house and he's annoying.

'And your mother – my God, there are times . . .'

'That's not what I mean. And, by the way, you never help!'

He looks nonplussed.

'Whenever they argue *I* always have to deal with it – you never do!'

While he's annoying me, a bitter row breaks out over the Plasticine. They both want the orange to make palm trees and are suddenly hurling it at each other. It ends with Lawrence clutching his head in pain and Lydia storming upstairs. For some reason Lawrence is furious with *me*.

'I'm not responsible for this,' I say.

'You shouldn't have children then!'

Seeing as I've produced a blamer *and* a sulker, I can only agree.

Later, Lydia comes back and apologizes, and I watch as they share out the Plasticine and continue playing.

'See?' says Peter. 'Everything's fine.'

And I know, I just *know*, that despite having done absolutely nothing as usual, he's going to take the credit. And sure enough, he picks up his newspaper, pops a piece of cheese into his mouth in the most unbelievably infuriating way, and says:

'Must be my influence.'

And then he looks surprised when I storm out.

Ages 9 & 10:
The Art of the Deal (1)

Now it's Christmas time, and the givin' ain't easy. Lydia's been leaving pictures cut out from her favourite reading matter, the Argos catalogue, wherever she thinks her father and I will pause long enough to memorize them: by the wine rack, mainly.

This year she's pining for the strangely named Teksta, apparently a horse-of-many-talents.

'You've already got a pony that can walk.'

This was Tawny, her undying favourite for about three days. Before him there was a Sindy pony bought on eBay, which lacked autonomous motion – rather like its owner at weekends – but had a nice face and came with a bridle and saddle, in a home-made box filled with real straw. And before that was the unicorn hobby horse whose cheek you pressed to make it neigh. All reside cheek by fetlock in Lydia's modestly sized bedroom.

'But this one can nuzzle you *and* neigh! It's touch and motion sensitive!'

In other words, more responsive than the average husband.

'But how long will you play with it for?'

'Forever! Please please please oh *please!*'

She even writes 'PLEASE PLEASE PLEASE OH *PLEASE*' in capitals along the margin of the ad.

Meanwhile Lawrence wants a PSP. He's never had a games console, which makes him, among his peer group, statistically unique.

'You've never asked us before. And you have managed without one all this time,' I point out.

'I was being *nice*.'

'Remember the CD players,' Peter intones.

Two Christmases ago, we gave them each a CD player. We'd had enough of the fights over the down-stairs stereo, with Lydia putting on *The Jungle Book* while Lawrence moaned all the way through it, demanding *The Best of Queen*.

But these big, exciting presents weren't the raging success we imagined.

Lydia got *Abba Gold* to go with hers, and does play it *occasionally*; I heard her singing along to 'Money, Money, Money' in her room the other day with a friend who'd come to play. But most of the time it just sits there.

So, while we are broadly in favour of any technology which buys us a bit of peace and quiet, you can see why we've so far resisted the lure of the Game Boy, the Xbox and the Wii. How do we know they'll actually play with them? And, absurd as it sounds, we quite like the sound of their little voices, even when it consists largely of:

'He won't let me have the red pencil!'

'She wouldn't give it to me first!'

And computer game homes are characterized by an eerie silence, broken only by the sound of bank statements being opened and weeping.

The other reason we have for not getting Lawrence a PSP is that Peter keeps referring to it as a 'PCP', i.e. the hallucinogenic drug popularly known as angel dust, briefly and lethally popular in American housing projects in the 1980s, which caused users to jump out of windows. So he cannot be trusted to go into shops.

However, he has lately begun to worry that we've gone too far and are starting to be a bit like those parents who don't allow television, only buy wooden toys and put their children in Birkenstocks.

I disagree. We allow unlimited television, have no wooden toys except Brio, and embarrass our kids by arguing with them in the chip shop about whether they're allowed a white roll while they wait for their fried carbs. Thus with almost no effort we are achieving the worst of both worlds: low standards *and* children who feel hard done by.

It's two weeks to Christmas. Time is running out!

We go trailing round town in a last-ditch attempt to find the ideal present for each child that isn't the unsuitable thing they actually want.

'I've got a radical idea,' I say, sinking into a chair in John Lewis, vacant probably because the previous occupant has gone to the toy department to commit suicide. 'How about we just stop struggling and give them the things they've asked for?'

'My God,' he says. 'It's radical all right!'

I can see his brain forming the thought, soon to become the words, *slippery slope*.

Because he grew up at a time when a lavish Christmas meant a pack of chocolate cigarettes and a slightly more colourful jumper, he's afraid of what might happen if we give our children – for want of a better word – a load of 'fancy' stuff. Because, as my father also felt about these things – where will it end? The idea lurks – if I'm honest, in *both* our minds – that once we give them battery-powered horses and games consoles, we'll be unable to avoid TVs in their rooms, karaoke machines, diamond ear studs and, ultimately, cars.

'My sister and I begged and begged for a talking doll,' I say. 'Where you pulled a string in its back to hear a series of deeply uninteresting phrases. And she became obsessed with getting a Katie Kopycat: a doll that sat opposite you and mimicked your actions.'

'Jesus, that sounds a bit ahead of its time.'

'I think she was just connected to this "magic desk" that came with her, and there were two pens joined together so when you wrote something, she "copied" it.'

Like: *Dear Mummy, if you don't buy me this doll I won't love you any more.*

Both my parents disapproved of toys like that because they left no room for the imagination; the more the toy did, the less there was for the child to make up.

And I'm sure they weren't the first. I bet every generation has its favourites that the masses rush out to buy in droves, but which a certain kind of middle-class parent refuses to get. You can just imagine an Ancient Greek telling her child:

'All right, you can have a slave. But no way are you getting one of these new-fangled spinning tops . . .'

So my mother held the line. She was a keen student of D.W. Winnicott – he of the 'good enough mother' – and read books with titles like *The Role of Play in Child Development*. She even took us to the Institute of Child Health to be observed playing behind a two-way mirror for one of their research projects, which has to be the poshest form of child-minding ever.

My father's position was just the effect of having grown up poor: what if you bought all these expensive toys and then became ill and lost your job, as happened to his father? I think sometimes when he lost his temper it was out of fear.

But he totally believed in fun. One year he got someone to make us a really big Wendy house – in plain brown hardwood, big enough for adults to stand up in if invited. And other kids' parents were appalled by the amount of mess we were allowed to make.

'When I was about four,' I tell Peter, 'we moved for a while to a flat that had an extra bedroom. Mum made it the playroom and gave us some Crazy Foam. We took all our clothes off and just sprayed it all over each other. I remember it vividly, sliding about on the lino, laughing hysterically.'

It occurs to me now that she should have grabbed that room for herself; I would have.

Peter's parents were even less keen on 'gimmicks', as they might have termed them, being a slightly earlier generation, who'd suffered not only rationing but the Depression as well.

'Basically, they were against anything with batteries.'

'So what did you plead for, that you didn't get?'

'When I was eight I wanted a Scalextric set.'

Can I just say I got him one as a wedding present.

'And what did you get?'

'I had Meccano, which was "educational". I did play with it a lot, though.'

And never lost a single piece. I don't know it yet, but in a few months the children will be up in his study using it; Lawrence to make a car, Lydia to build a toy animal enclosure. It may be educational, but don't hold that against it.

'Why not Scalextric, though?'

'Because "it's just cars going round and round" . . . And, in those days, motor racing was incredibly dangerous, not like now.'

The year he was born saw the worst accident in racing history: eighty-four people were killed.

'But you weren't planning to actually *be* a racing driver, were you? And besides, Scalextric requires some skill and focusing and is *fun*.'

I found the adrenalin rush and the level of

concentration it demanded really absorbing and thus an excellent de-stresser, even though despite practising a fair bit I've never managed to accelerate *and* keep the car on the track. In the coming years I will be beaten several times by my eight-year-old nephew.

Peter's ramblings may sound irrelevant, as they so often do, but then I think, the fear of My Little Overdraft is definitely part of it, and also *control*: a bit of us wants them to be nine and ten forever, playing sweetly with the gifts we choose.

A sales assistant comes over and asks if we're thinking of buying the chair.

Peter hauls me up.

'Maybe we *should* get them those things,' he says. 'They don't ask for much. And we might get tons of brownie points.'

'And,' I say, 'Lydia says she'll play with that horse forever and ever and *EVER*. So she won't need anything next year.'

So we do.

And Lydia plays with it once.

And Lawrence plays with the PSP a *lot*, but it won't save his scores. So we take it back to John Lewis. And they tell me to either buy a memory stick or complain to Sony, which is not what the Sale of Goods Act says, not remotely. And instead of arguing with them, which I know will distress him, I give in and hate myself.

So it's not getting the PSP which has turned out to be a Key Stage, but seeing his mother offering to solve a problem, claiming to be his protector and champion – and failing to do so. He will have lost faith in me. All this trouble we've gone to, not having Father Christmas, and explaining that ads are fiction, and telling the truth about death – that was supposed to establish our integrity. And I've undone it all. And he's too young; this sort of disillusionment shouldn't happen for ages yet.

But here I am again, thinking that all these stages are supposed to be at a certain point – always a point in the future, instead of handling them when they do happen, i.e. today: *now.*

'I'm so sorry,' I tell him, over a rather good chicken and avocado ciabatta in the cafe. 'I'm not sure what we should do.'

He chews thoughtfully.

'It's OK,' he says. 'I think I might just put it up for sale in the school newsletter.'

I search his face for signs of a complete collapse of faith in the female parent, but he looks fine.

As for me, I have to confront the discovery that John Lewis isn't the all-giving, all-nurturing meeter of my needs I believed it was, that delivers where other shops fail, and always cares.

So you could say we both moved on a stage today.

After he ate most of the Christmas chocolate teddy she was given and broke her trust in adults forever, Peter bought Lydia a giant Toblerone to make up for it.

And now he has weakened *again*, and eaten five sections of that self-same Toblerone.

It'll be all the more shocking for her when she finds out, as he's the parent with the willpower. And he'll have to go back to square one to rebuild her trust in him and regain his position as the Nice One. I am sorry for her, but pleased to see him in trouble for a change. Except he hasn't owned up.

'I'll take the blame if you like,' says Lawrence.

'Will you really?'

'Yeah. It'll cost you a quid.'

Peter looks haunted, like a desperate prisoner who only wanted a pillow and is now in hock to the biggest hard man on the wing.

It isn't just the price he sets for taking the rap that bothers me, it's the speed of the response, as if he's used to making deals in dark parking lots in a hurry, before the Feds arrive. Despite our efforts to seal the perimeter while we've been watching all eighty-two episodes of *The Sopranos*, I fear some of the ethics may have seeped up through the ceiling into our son's room. Last summer he sold me a pebble for 50p – a really nice round one to add to my collection, but he knows I have an addiction. And it was unsettling. Are we breeding a creative entrepreneur who'll survive whatever hellish challenges the future has in store, or a proto Alan Sugar?

After Lawrence sold the PSP, we agreed he would perform useful household tasks in return for cash to put towards a – considerably more expensive – Wii. Because the way to put a bad game console experience behind you is obviously to get another one.

Precisely what these tasks would be led to negotiations which rumbled on through the summer like one of those industrial disputes which lasted most of the 1970s.

Finally we agreed that he would start by cleaning the car for £10: £5 for the outside and £5 for the interior.

But he takes a strangely long time to get started.

'I'm a bit hungry,' he says on the first morning.

Then, after breakfast he can't start because he has to 'help Lydia find Pinky the Bear', which would be sweet if it weren't for the fact that Lydia loses things quite a bit, and devoting any time to helping her find them basically means saying goodbye to your week. Also, though she doesn't know it yet, when we took Pinky on holiday to Italy, he fell for the sun-drenched, early-retirement-on-full-pension lifestyle and decided not to come back.

That takes Lawrence till lunch, after which he disappears with his sketchbook:

'You know how you like me to draw.'

After that, he says helpfully:

'I should probably watch that DVD so you can send it back.'

We get three films a week in the post from LoveFilm, enabling us to claim – quite truthfully – that we now watch very little television.

'DVD *after* car cleaning,' I say.

'Can I watch it?' says Lydia.

'No.'

At 10 a.m. the next day I say,

'All ready to clean the car?'

'I've got hypoglycaemia,' he says. 'I need to eat first.'

He has recently had breakfast of bacon, eggs and beans.

'You know it's real, Mummy: you get it too.'

This is true. I could ignore it, but when he does indeed get low blood sugar he behaves like me with

PMT, only worse. It provoked the most terrifying outbursts of temper in my father before almost every meal, so I am quite keen to get him managing it early in life. I shove a piece of shortbread in his hand and point him towards the sink.

In comes Peter, features screwed up with concern.

'Have you got any moisturizer?' he says. 'It's all this housework I'm doing. I've got "dishpan hands".'

The children have never seen the old Lux ads, so don't react, and I have seen them, but ignore him.

He spots the bucket on the draining board, waiting to be filled: the extent of Lawrence's progress so far.

'Excellent work! Well done.'

'He hasn't even started yet, for God's sake,' I mutter.

'I'm just being encouraging: you should try it.'

'Fuck off, why don't you? Jesus.'

Lawrence bends halfway to the cupboard where we keep the washing-up liquid, and stops.

'Did you know,' he says, 'that statistically, you're more likely to be eaten by leopards than win the lottery?'

'And did *you* know,' I say, 'that by the time you've washed the car and saved up the money to buy it, the Wii will be obsolete. You'll have to go and look at it in a museum.'

We open the cupboard and spend quite a while sifting through the extensive collection of used and semi-used cloths, scraps of old T-shirt for dusting and two tins of saddle soap that someone lent us in 2001 to clean the seats of a car we no longer have.

Eventually, I manage to shove him outside with the bucket and the cloths, and he *finally* cleans the car.

'Nice job,' I say. 'Here's your money.'

Then it rains.

'I think it's really good for them to learn to do this stuff,' says Peter. 'I used to wash my father's Rover. And I didn't even get paid.'

As he muses smugly on his Ladybird book past, Lydia comes in.

'Anyone know what happened to my Toblerone?'

Silence.

'Daddy, I'm looking at *you*.'

Hah!

I've had to put up with being the flawed parent all these years; it's about time he was exposed as non-perfect Peter so they can be disappointed in him too. Then – *yes!* – Lydia shakes her head and actually says it.

'I'm just really disappointed in you.'

Me: 1, Peter: 0, Child Development: 2. He looks crushed. She doesn't look too thrilled either.

Of course, she wouldn't have reacted like this if I'd done it, because I've planned ahead by disappointing them from the very start.

Lost and Found

I am walking Lawrence up to his friend Milo's, a few minutes away. When we arrive, Milo's dad tells the boys they can go to the park together – without him.

So far we've been theoretically supporting the children's progress to independence by discussing it without doing too much about it, a strategy of Peter's. They've both been down to the shop a few times to spend their pocket money, but as there are no roads to cross, it's hardly a major challenge. Yet in the current climate there are parents who won't let their ten-year-olds do even that. And the less they do, the less they're able to do.

But – every time I visualize them in the outside world without us, my imagination conjures up a long wait followed by a visit from the police, their hats respectfully removed to denote Very Bad News.

So I'm relieved that the park decision has been taken out of my hands. And if they do come to any

71

harm it'll be on the other guy's watch. This thought is most reassuring.

Also, I am fairly certain that Lawrence has absorbed my instructions on what to do if approached by a creepy stranger. But obviously, I must make sure.

'They'll sound very plausible,' I tell him. 'They'll say something like, "Your mum sent me to get you," but they'll be lying.'

'I know. You told me *a million times*.'

'You scream, shout, hurt them as much as possible, then run to a shop or the park cafe and get them to phone the police.'

'Scream, kick, phone. I *know*. Can I go now?'

With Lydia I'm not so sure. The same instructions produce this response:

'But what if it's Jessica?'

Jessica is Peter's sister.

'No, obviously not. Someone you *don't* know.'

'What if it's Katarina?'

Katarina used to be their nanny. She lives nearby and still babysits.

'No! Someone you DON'T KNOW! For God's sake, Lydia!'

Because of her ability to turn a simple brief into a Socratic dialogue, I have to keep reiterating it to see how much – if any – has sunk in. I test her on it after school, at bedtime, before and after homework, and still I have no idea whether she's heard. It all comes of having too much imagination. When I first tried to teach her the road-crossing drill, she said:

'I wouldn't *mind* being run over, if it was by an ice-cream van.'

So you can see what we're up against.

All goes well and Lawrence returns from his unsupervised park visit unscathed.

'You see?' says Peter. 'I told you he'd be fine.'

A few days later, he and Lydia are at the park, and I'm working at home, when I get a text:

Lyd lost. If not back in 20 mins will call u.

This provokes a cocktail of emotions: fear, anxiety and the smidgen of relief that whatever happens, it'll be her father's fault.

Ten minutes later she has appeared.

'She was very good actually,' he says, when they get back. 'She went to the cafe to ask if she could borrow a phone to ring me, but there was a queue, and then I turned up anyway.'

'Very good, Lydia!' I say. 'That was exactly the right thing to do.'

Though I do rather wish she'd jumped the queue on the grounds that it was an emergency.

Of course, she was facing an additional challenge,

on which she has not been briefed. Peter often isn't where he says he's going to be, so it's easy to 'get lost' without going anywhere. She and I once spent half a boiling hot afternoon waiting for him in the basement of the Science Museum – with no phone signal – while he 'went upstairs for a minute' and was gone for two hours.

When he eventually did reappear I wanted to drown him in the water play table, but it was all witnessed by those nice young staff they have called Explainers, who can decode any phenomenon in the known universe except why my husband always says, 'I'll meet you back here in twenty minutes,' and then disappears for two hours. But let's deal with one thing at a time.

Handily, an opportunity to learn a bit of self-reliance has arisen in the form of the Year Five canoeing trip. This time, Lawrence will be paddling and cooking in twos and threes, like *The Apprentice* meets *Bridge Over the River Kwai*, though if he loses his paddle he won't be hauled in front of the teacher and ritually drowned. Mind you, I haven't been through the small print.

He's been told to bring a small, light bag with 'just the essentials', then I turn over the page to find a kit list that makes Shackleton's attempt on the Antarctic look like a weekend in Paris. I borrow alien items like *bivvy bags* – huge waterproof sachets – from families who do this sort of thing willingly in their free time, and we lay it all out on his bed. It's impressive, though to me more for gazing at in wonder than actually using, like a double-page spread from a Dorling Kindersley book.

And this is only the small stuff; the canoes, tents, Trangias – not an East European car, I discover, but a portable stove – are being provided by the school. Lawrence is alight with anticipation. He can't wait to hear the rush of the current, feel the Welsh breeze on his face and go four days without touching a bar of soap. Also, they're invited to bring matches and a knife. And if *that* isn't thrilling enough, he'll be consorting with boys from Year Seven and even Eight.

'This is a big leap forward,' says Peter.

'I know: they'll be expected to wash up their own plates.'

The day before he leaves, it finally sinks in that my precious ten-year-old is about to get into a very small floating container with two other boys – who could be sensible, but on the other hand might well muck about and capsize it – on a large body of moving water, 180 miles from home. I can feel the pull of the outside world, like a powerful force, clutching at my baby! I shouldn't have watched so many films where spaceships get pulled into magnetic fields and don't come back.

To ward off anxiety I distract myself with the fine detail: for instance, the fact that the word 'cagoule' is spookily similar to Gagool, the name of the evil toothless crone in *King Solomon's Mines*. This is more effective than you might think.

Then he's gone.

The four days pass more quickly than I expect, and quite calmly, except for Peter coming in about twice a day and gasping,

'Just think! Our little Lawrence! On a river!'

It only occurs to me much later that he's celebrating it as something *good*.

On the fourth night our explorer returns, triumphant: tanned, grubby and with his toothbrush in exactly the same position as he packed it, the hair I placed, James Bond-style across the handle, still in place. And he sounds different.

'Blimey, I think his voice has broken,' says Peter. But no, it's only the effect of yelling to his mates in the other boats.

'Look at this, Mummy.'

He shows me the sharp stick he whittled.

'Wow, what was *that* for?'

'We stuck our marshmallows on it.'

'Wow. What else?'

'We ate cold pasta.'

'Gosh.'

'Halfway through cooking, the stove went out.'

The thrill! Then just before he zooms off to sleep he murmurs,

'Rapids . . .'

'What?'

'We went down them on our backs. It was *great*!'

In the morning I ask him:

'Do you feel different?'

'Yeah,' he says. 'Older. Like I can do more.'

'Great!' I say, unpacking the sticky plates. 'I think you're now ready to learn the vital life skill of how to wash up.'

This will take another eight years.

Understanding the Facts of Life

After lunch during one of her rare visits to London, my friend Janet announces she has one vital thing to buy before she gets the train.

'I'll come with you,' I say. 'What do you have to get?'

But of course she's not shopping for herself.

'I need to buy a sex education book for the kids.'

She's told them the 'nitty-gritty', as she puts it. But there's something far trickier to be tackled. Matthew is starting to *change*.

'He's getting into major teenage-style strops,' she explains. 'And—'

'And?'

'His armpits are starting to smell!'

He's only nine.

We go into a bookshop, and ask in loud, clear voices:

'Have you got any books on sex?'

'For children.'

'We mean the Facts of Life – you know.'

'It's funny,' says Janet, 'if we were asking for ourselves we'd whisper.'

Nonetheless, the sales assistants seem confused by our request and it takes three of them to steer us to the right section. I once returned a picture book about making babies by a popular and excellent author because it referred euphemistically to 'egg-laying'. And, while Daddy had a willy – tiny, but at least visible – poor Mummy had just a blank space: literally nada. Nowadays, do children think there's something wrong with them if they're not like the picture? Surely they do look at themselves. Still, I must vet Janet's choices.

We both like one which takes a sort of *Horrible Histories* approach, with cartoons of many variations on the human figure – 'nobody's perfect' – but find ourselves distracted by searching for our own shapes.

'Hmm,' she says, 'Trinny and Susannah should do one of these.'

'It'd be miles better than *The Joy of Sex* we all read in the seventies, with those awful hairy drawings.'

Pretty much all I can remember about it is the endless *beards*.

'Which were obviously a covert strategy to put teenagers off sex.'

'Well, it worked.'

'For a while, anyway.'

Eventually we pull ourselves out of our reminiscences as Janet must make a decision or miss her train. She chooses *Puberty: Boy*; the companion volume *Puberty: Girl* will later suit her seven-year-old. Being stingier, I get one for Lawrence and Lydia to share: Usborne's *Understanding the Facts of Life*, which is informative, friendly and not twee. We went over the basics two years ago during the ad break in *Friends*, when they came into the room just as Rachel confessed she'd slept with her ex, Barry the Dentist. And as I didn't want to miss any of the second half I explained it really quickly, and forgot to say you can get pregnant.

'So it was all over too soon, just like a first sexual experience!' said Peter, very pleased with himself.

When I get home, I try to stimulate interest in my new purchase.

'I've got this really great book for you . . .' I begin.

'Not *again* . . .'

'You're always forcing us to read *books*!'

'But this one's really interesting. It's about sex.'

Lawrence sighs.

'We've *done* sex. We had to watch a video. It went on for *twenty minutes*.'

I try for a bit longer, then leave it on the kitchen

counter and wait till bathtime, when I work the conversation round to Matthew's armpits. It's a bit of a swerve from Hadrian's Wall and the six times table, but using outrageous Radio 4-style links I get there in the end.

'You'll change,' I tell them. 'You'll get hair here and here, and' – looking at Lawrence now – 'your voice will get deeper.'

'Awww!' says Lydia. 'I like my voice.'

'Not *you*: you get the bosoms.'

'Ha ha!' says Lawrence.

Somehow I've managed to spin it so neither is happy with their lot.

And anyway, Lawrence is only really concerned about his height. I tell him my father was only five foot seven and it never held him back, but since Lawrence never met him it means nothing; I may as well be talking about Napoleon. So I explain that not everyone develops the same way or even at the same rate; there are boys in his year with size nine feet who look as though they've grown out of their uniforms since lunch. Even so, he is still the second shortest in the class, a fact that has made us somewhat relaxed about getting him new clothes. We just noticed he's been having trouble getting his school polo shirt off at night; when he took it off for the last time you could actually see his chest expand. The label said '*Age 5–6*'.

'At least now we know why he's smaller than the rest of the class,' said Peter.

Two days later I come down to find the children reading the book together: result!

And from sex it is but a short step to drugs.

Lawrence is doing them already. He's only in Year Five so it's all happening rather sooner than I expected.

The first I hear of it is when he asks me if I know what heroin looks like.

'Er, I'm not sure. Sort of brown, I think. Why?'

'I've got to draw it for my homework.'

He shows me his exercise book. There's a cup, some roundish dots, a cigarette packet, a couple of slightly wobbly-looking sticks and something that looks a bit like a very small molehill next to a hypodermic.

'That's coffee, that's aspirin, those are cigarettes, that's two joints, and that's heroin.'

'Very good!' I say. 'Lovely syringe.'

I'm particularly glad to see the cigarettes.

'They kill more people than anything! We saw a video of a man and his lungs were all black.'

'Urgh! And I met a man who smoked so much he had to have his tongue removed.'

This, sad to say, is true. But will Lawrence remember it when the time comes?

'But I need *more* drugs, Mummy,' he says.

'Let's see . . . There's heroin and LSD and cocaine, um, amphetamines . . .'

The names come to mind in a kind of rhythmic canter, like Tom Lehrer's song about the periodic table: *he-ro-in and L-S-D, am-phe-ta-mines and ecs-sta-seee* . . . I don't sing this out loud.

'Cocaine's quite popular,' I say vaguely.

'What does that do to you, Mummy?'

'I think it makes you talk too fast and believe you sound much cleverer than you actually are.'

In other words, like me all the time.

'So obviously I've never felt the need to take it. Or ecstasy. It comes on little bits of paper sometimes with smileys on. And LSD. Do some smileys and you've got them both covered.'

At this his credulity is strained.

'Bits of paper! What's the point of those?!'

'You eat them. The paper is impregnated with the drug.'

He snorts derisively.

'What are they meant to do, anyway?'

I stop – not my instinctive response during most conversations – and think.

I've never ingested these two substances either. But here I am, presented with a golden opportunity to influence my child's future! He's at the stage where all this is still hypothetical. And although I know that this information will probably never come to mind when he's jumping about to music in a field with ten thousand others, it's impossible not to hope that it will, just a tiny bit. The description I'm about to offer could make the difference between life and death one day. I say 'one day' to make it sound further off in time than it actually is. In as little as seven years he could be in a tent or a nightclub stairwell about to make a life-changing chemical decision. And here I am, imagining that I have a smidgen of control over the outcome.

Because, is he, in all likelihood, ever going to say:

'I would have a couple of Es off you, except my mum says they might kill me. Have you got any Kit-Kats?'

'Well, Mummy?!'

'Er . . . what? Oh, right. Ecstasy makes you love everybody but it can kill you, er, in some unlucky instances, and, er, LSD makes you see things that aren't there, often in quite a scary way.'

The former heroin addict I briefly went out with in the eighties told me he was more frightened by acid than anything – aside from his mother.

'Right,' says Lydia, 'I'm definitely not having *that*.'

Excellent.

'Unless I can see something really *nice*, like ponies.'

'Right . . . Can you both clear up now for supper?'

But Lawrence gestures again at his book.

'We're supposed to have thirty.'

'*Thirty?!*'

'We did thirty drugs in the lesson.'

'Gosh,' I say. 'I probably know about eight or ten, but thirty . . .'

'Remember, it includes cigarettes and caffeine and stuff.'

Phew. We sit down.

'Did you know caffeine's quite bad for you?'

'Well, yes. I do try not to drink too much coff—'

'And alcohol. You drink quite a lot of wine, don't you?'

'Er. Well. A fair bit, yes.'

Has this child ever had any illusions?

I'm sure he's always known the Tooth Fairy and I had the same handwriting – not to mention a similar tendency to have a few drinks then fall into bed without delivering his pound. He's a natural sceptic, and therefore, I decide, less likely ever to fall under the spell of drug dealers. This cheers me considerably, although the thought occurs that he and his classmates have been eagerly putting up their hands to tell the teacher whose parents drink the most.

'And – are you listening, Mummy? We're allowed to include paracetamol and things like that.'

'Oh! Well, in that case . . .'

I reel off a list of every painkiller known to woman. Peter comes in.

'What are you up to?'

'We're just spelling *diazepam*.'

'Jolly good! Drink?'

'Yes please.'

'It's your favourite drug, isn't it Mummy?'

It is indeed – apart from sugar. If chips and choc-olate weren't legal – and they frankly shouldn't be – I'd have to hang around in alleys flogging stolen phones for £5 wraps of Dairy Milk. We know the children aren't that keen on sweets, one reason we've been able to steal their Easter eggs; they've been known to leave chocolate unattended for months. Peter has occasional binges such as the chocolate teddy, but is otherwise not a slave to his appetites. Clearly the most addictive personality in the house is mine – so we can stop worrying.

In and Out the Pupa

That summer we go on holiday to Italy, where Lydia is stung by a wasp and doesn't cry. As I'm marvelling at this, she smooths on some anti-sting lotion and says:

'You may think I handled that rather well, Mummy, but it was in fact only a baby wasp.'

And yes, I know 'baby wasps' are actually larvae which can't fly – but *handled*? Where is she getting this disconcertingly mature mode of expression? It's not in the books. We all know to expect them to start getting bigger in some places and growing hair in others; no one tells you what to do when they start talking like Paul McKenna.

She is after all only nine, and still using travel not to broaden her horizons but to increase her vast collection of fluffy toys. Have you ever stood in an airport and wondered what sort of person ignores the little models of, say, the Colosseum or Leaning Tower to commemorate their holiday to Italy, in favour of a cuddly hedgehog holding a plaque inscribed with their star sign? Well, now you know.

Then at supper one night we're all talking away as usual, and, bursting to say something, she *puts up her hand*. She even holds it up with the other one and presses her lips together while signalling 'Pick me!' with her eyes.

Plus we've gone on holiday with other people, which changes things again, because whatever stage they're at, children are hugely influenced by the company they're in. Well, aren't we all? We were once invited to lunch in a massive house filled with grand pianos and priceless sculptures, whose owner demonstrated how to tiptoe – actually mimed Very Careful Walking, like a pantomime villain – so they wouldn't crash into any of the valuables. So we were all quite surprised when their children threw food, and Lawrence and Lydia – evidently not wanting to be rude – followed suit.

In Italy we're staying with a nine-, a thirteen- and a three-year-old, so it could go either way. But I've reckoned without the place itself, which exerts its own civilizing influence. With the exception of a rogue Coke-ordering incident – the downside of putting all the kids on their own table – they behave beautifully.

'Well done for being so grown up,' Peter and I gush proudly in the car afterwards, about two seconds before hysterics erupt in the back. I've been urging them to learn some new words, but this is definitely not what I had in mind.

'Ha ha!' shrieks Lydia. 'I'm a shag!'

Peter immediately shoots me an accusing look, like the respectable citizen who automatically blames everything on the problem family down the road.

'No, Lydia,' says Lawrence, 'shag's a verb, a *doing* word.'

I say to their father,

'Aren't they meant to be growing out of this phase?'

'She seems to be growing *into* it.'

Why can't they develop like normal species? You don't get caterpillars becoming butterflies for a bit, then going back into their pupae and coming out again as caterpillars. If you plotted her mental maturity on a graph it would be like a series of Hokusai waves: going up and curling back, then down again.

I suppose they're like those friction cars you have to pull into reverse and let go; it's simply how they're designed.

Our friend Angela says one reason independence doesn't happen in a strictly linear fashion is that the separation process is more of a long-term, evolving thing.

'How long term?'

'Well, one of mine still didn't want me to wave to him when we met at the theatre for his birthday last month.'

'How could you tell?'

'The way he stood, really, when he saw me across the foyer, with his arms pinned to his sides.'

He's twenty-eight.

Maybe she has a particularly strange wave.

But then, *our* desires aren't straightforward either. We want them to grow out of reciting rude words in the back of the car, but not to stop curling up on our laps. At times I want them to stay this age forever, a feeling that evaporates whenever I find it's taken me an hour just to get them into bed.

And, again in the car, we overhear this:

'And then rum . . . sugar and mint.'

I hiss at Peter:

'That's how to make a mojito!'

He laughs, quietly so they don't hear.

I turn round.

'Are you telling your little sister how to make a mojito? How do you know what goes *in* a mojito?'

'I've had one,' he says casually.

'What?! *Where?*'

'Oh, I don't know. In a bar somewhere.'

*

When we come back from holiday, things seem to calm down.

'Could we go shopping together one day?' Lydia says.

This is it! The First Mother-and-Daughter Shopping Day Milestone – well, apart from shouting at each other in the bridesmaids' section of BHS.

Though I am waging a – largely futile – campaign to get her to save rather than spend, I really feel quite moved. Only recently I was in M&S and passing the 'first bra' section, felt a lump in my throat: just a 30AA lump, but still.

'Oh yes!' I say. 'We can have a lovely day together.'

'We could go to the Build a Bear shop!'

Ah.

This is the current girl craze. They go to a party where a woman hands out teddy bears with little hearts inside their chests that you can remove, or put in, or something – though not in a cool or even educational way – and clothes and accessories, from strangely wide tops and shorts to sunglasses. And 'birth certificates' with the child's name on as parent. The typography is truly horrible.

It costs the host's parents I don't know what, and afterwards the child comes home and makes you go to the Build a Bear *shop* and ruin yourself. So, basically they're Tupperware parties for six- to nine-year-olds, except that no one ever burst into tears because they hadn't got every single size of plastic vegetable storer. Actually, maybe some people did. I collect spherical pebbles, so who am I to talk.

'No, Lydia,' I say. 'Because you've got two already,' not to mention a stack of their bizarre accoutrements like flip-flops – they don't have *toes* – 'and soon you'll grow out of that and wish you'd spent the money on something else.'

Suddenly she is furious.

'I'll NEVER GROW OUT OF BUILD A BEAR – *NEVER!!*'

And she storms out.

'This is all part of testing the boundaries,' says my mother.

'Yeah, but couldn't she just ask where they are? This is *knackering*.'

She laughs supportively, but I get off the phone before she starts telling me what I was like at that age.

The thing is, it really is exactly like an argument with a teenager, really *exactly*. The terrible thought recurs: what if childhood *is* adolescence? The *whole bloody thing*?

When they're little they adore you, even – though

it may not seem it – through the tantrum stage. You've brought them into the world, are the source of their entire life-sustaining universe, and you know everything. Then they discover they can gain knowledge that you don't have.

'Mummy, did you know that three times three is nine?'

'Gosh, is it really? I never knew that.'

Or, if you're Lawrence – in Year Five:

'Lydia . . . did you know that the angle of the average erection is 160 degrees?'

Which is the sort of detail you get from PSHE these days.

But it happens much sooner than that.

We just don't realize it.

Maybe that's because we're looking at the wrong things.

What if we paid less attention to Key Stage One and other academic issues and continued more in the vein of nursery schools? So they start with learning how to use the loo, how to line up for lunch, sit down quietly and listen and so on. Then reading, of course, and counting. And drawing. Oh, and loving Nature, the way we did before it became the Environment. Then they go onto the next level of vital abilities that will sustain them for life.

I don't know why Lydia decided to draw a line under the argument with Poppy, or how Lawrence was able to shrug off the punch in the lunch queue. It's an invaluable skill, one that I would give anything to have had – to have now. And perhaps that – along with the arguing and the incredibly tiresome stubbornness – is how they grow up.

So later on, instead of worrying so much about whether they'll be doing ten GCSEs or be first violin or the lead in the school play, we could notice if they've learned how to negotiate, or to disagree with their friends without falling out, or to expend less of their energy on the effort to be *popular*. And if you think that's a side issue, ask any woman over thirty-five how many unnecessary things she's done in her life just to be liked.

Each moment, with every single spark of their energy, they're focused on gaining the skills to become independent beings who – one, not so far-off day – won't need us. And this might be part of that.

Am I saying we should all roll over and rejoice in our kids being impossible? Not at all: if we don't argue back they tend to find more spectacular ways to rebel.

Two's a Crowd

The children used to deploy numerous creative strategies to try and get to stay up later:

'Would you like a foot rub, Mummy? You know you like them.'

'Oh, what's that book? I *love* books.'

'Would you like another glass of wine? Shall I get it?'

And the old standby:

'I love you, Mummy! You're the Best Mummy in the World.'

A mere year or so on, however, they no longer need to. They are so energetic, and we are so worn out, that the unthinkable has happened: last Saturday we fell asleep before them.

As with so many of these stages, it's happened far sooner than we expected. To paraphrase John Lennon, growing up is what they do while you're reading books on child development.

We blunder around looking for voices breaking

and bosoms burgeoning, deciding that if we don't see them, our kids must be the same as they were last year. But they're not. We're just missing the subtle indicators that show us the true picture.

We had a classic example this week. Having hitherto enjoyed only a superficial acquaintance with the hairbrush, leading to shouting matches on the doorstep every time we left the house, Lydia had not only brushed and tied back her hair, but fallen asleep clutching the formerly reviled object. I called Peter in and we stood transfixed together over her recumbent form, like Howard Carter discovering Tutankhamun with his golden flail. Her previously preferred night-time companion, the disturbingly lipsticked Build a Bear, now lay on the floor with its skirt up.

'It brings a lump to the throat,' said Peter.

And as development indicators go, it beats the hell out of flouncing and door slamming.

So not only do internal and external changes not always happen in sync, there's a sort of zigzag pattern to it. For example, Lydia's allowed to go to school by herself now if she wants to; it's a short walk with only one scary main road and Doug, the nice lollipop man, to see her across. I've already embarrassed her by snapping at drivers using mobiles and telling some of the older girls to wait for the green man. The older girls! So going alone would bring at least two benefits. She'd gain more independence and I wouldn't be there to show her up. Also, I'd get more time in bed.

But she doesn't always want to. Or she wants to go on her bike, which is too small. When she pedals her knees hit the handlebars. But when I said, 'We'll consider it,' She said: 'Well, *I've* considered it and I've said Yes.'

And then later, when it flared up again:

'I've taken your comments into account.'

As for Lawrence, he's showing no signs of the rejection he should be inflicting on me about now, when boys are meant to reinforce their masculinity by shifting away from their mother towards their father. If anything, he's oddly polite.

When we meet a neighbour in the street and I tell him to say hello, he says:

'Mum, I think we can safely say I've passed the point now where you need to tell me to do this.'

See what I mean?

And he's right. The 'say hello' reflex is one of the habits I've got from my mother. It's not even conscious. I don't find myself thinking: 'I must start doing all the things she did that irritated me when I was that age.' It's just preloaded, like a game on your phone you don't want.

I'm getting the same amount of affection as ever.

But one evening, I perceive a change. A cheery irony has lately begun to creep in. When I said,

'Put your dirty plate in the sink, will you?'

He said,

'I already have. We call that "putting it in the sink".'

Note that the sink is as far it got.

And he's refusing to share his core skills with us, as in when he found the channel we wanted on our fiendishly clever new TV recorder – sales slogan: 'You can record anything in the known universe but can't watch it.'

'Tell us what you did! I demand to know!'

And he said, over his shoulder:

'Jog on.'

'Is that some new phrase they're all using?' said Peter, sounding about a hundred and two.

But we will soon be longing for the sunlit uplands of the cheery sarcasm phase.

'You know how I said he's not rejecting me as boys are meant to do around puberty?'

'Because he's only ten.'

'Well, he's doing it now.'

'What, since yesterday?'

'Yup.'

He's arguing back a lot, and with rather a limited repertoire of insults, like bad talk radio. Our worst exchanges bear a dispiriting resemblance to those I had with my mother when I was a teenager. Except he is indeed only ten.

'Lawrence, would you like some tea?'

'Mmnh.'

'Sorry?'

'I said *no*.'

'No *thank you*.'

'Whatever.'

In my day kids had the decency to wait until adolescence before becoming obnoxious. Now, no one waits until fourteen or even thirteen; they want to be obnoxious *now*. What will they have to look forward to?

Little do I know.

It certainly reminds me why we had two children, so that when one's being hideous you can transfer your affections to the other. Though no stranger to flouncing and door slamming, Lydia is currently being the Good One. She sits at the table drawing 'Mummy as an Angel' and Being Nice.

'Are you all right, Mummy?' she says, finding me yet again with my head in my hands.

'Lawrence is just being really rude to me at the moment,' I say.

'He's getting to that stage where he's starting to have an attitude,' she says thoughtfully. 'A *bad* attitude.'

Then, when we're discussing arrangements for the end of term, I notice that on the last day, they finish at different times.

'Oh, look,' I say, because I don't think before I speak. 'Lydia finishes at noon, and you finish at 12.30.'

Lawrence is outraged.

'So she gets half an hour *more holiday than me*?!'

Yes, he really says this. Are these the Pettiest Children in Britain? It's like being the owner of the world's longest fingernails. You know you've wasted your life, but at least you're famous for something.

Looking back, I think maybe it was a mistake to stop at two. People I've known from large families have had their piggy banks raided and food stolen off their plates by older siblings, yet emerged surprisingly unscathed. I've even met a one-of-five who missed out on a Christmas stocking one year following a miscount. Yet he doesn't hold a grudge; if anything he's more resilient, more able to withstand life's knocks.

So because fours, fives and sixes are continually

shoved aside and lost in the crowd they never *expect* life to be fair, whereas being one of two, with its futile expectation of equality, affords endless opportunities for disappointment.

Peter once read an interview with a famous novelist who as a child threw himself to the floor and sobbed because his brother had been given a biscuit. And our old friend Alison's two boys once argued all the way from Watford to Stockton because one had looked out of the other's window.

Now I can't think *why* I specifically wanted two, as my sister and I were awful. We drove our mother to the brink almost every day, constantly on the lookout for infinitesimal signs of favouritism, and waged wars over nothing.

Friends who came to play had to wait as glasses of lemonade, pieces of cake etc., were held up and scru-tinized for minuscule discrepancies in volume or size, something that no one else seemed to find necessary. Christmas presents were also exactly the same, with variations only in colour: red for me, blue for her. And bathtime was a minefield, taken up less with washing than interminable manoeuvrings of the chrome soap 'bridge' we used as a border control. The wall was tiled and the bath eleven tiles long, so we were each entitled to exactly five and a half tiles of space, minus the width of the soap bridge. All would go well until one of us moved the bridge, either deliberately or accidentally, and Mum would come in to find us angrily pushing and pulling it back and forth by distances of about half an inch, while more and more water got on the floor. It was basically the Middle East with seven-year-olds.

And we used to wonder why she went on dates with such dull men. Who wouldn't want to dress up and sit in a clean, tidy restaurant where other people cooked and served dinner, to a soundtrack of something other than yelling?

But of course I thought when I had my own children it would be different. We knocked them out fourteen months apart chiefly to prevent those sorts of petty rivalries. It helps a bit that Lawrence can't remember a time before Lydia, so he never became accustomed to life as the centre of the universe as I did for those three glorious years.

But despite these precautions the two of them currently come home from school every day to fight over the computer, and when told to share it, to battle over the central position on the bench seat.

It makes you want to scream. Humans' greatest evolutionary achievement is surely the art of negotiation, and at this rate I can't see how they're ever going to learn it. If they ever get as far as the world of work, they'll end up complaining because the person next to them has a smoother swivel chair. Or they'll turn out like the woman who complained at the swimming pool the other day that I was going round 'the wrong way' when I'd simply followed the guy in front of me, and besides, there were only three of us in there.

Peter says they'll grow out of it, that no phase lasts forever.

'So? That's precisely why we're always struggling to keep up. Because it keeps bloody changing!'

'Babyhood was exhausting,' he admits. 'But that was replaced by the toddler years . . .'

'Which were *also* exhausting.'

'Exactly. And then that phase gave way to the start of school . . .'

'Exhausting *again*.' Although they were at least out for part of the day. 'So what you're saying is, all we have to do is sit tight and wait for the next phase of being constantly wrong-footed and worn out. Great.'

I've gone off my new theory about adolescence: it's too tiring.

Ages 10 & 11:
Expandable by up to 20 per cent

Just as we're finishing dinner, Peter and I have a huge argument and I storm upstairs. I assume the children will take his side, but Lydia rushes up to the bedroom after me and curls up on my pillow, stroking my face. Then Lawrence comes up and rubs my feet. What lovely, supportive children. Nyeah to you, Husband!

'Thank you so much,' I say. 'You are lovely.'

And Lawrence says:

'I think you should probably see a psychiatrist.'

Oh.

'Actually I'm fine now, thank you darling. I feel much better.'

You should have seen me before.

'Seriously, it really is getting worse.'

'I'm sorry. I'm fine now. Sorry.'

'Look,' he says. 'Relax and breathe slowly. That-a-at's it. Better?'

'Much!'

'That's a classic relaxation technique,' I say. 'Where did you learn it?'

'School.'

Never mind French and Biology: this is a Major Life Skill. I've gone from shaking and growling to being all floppy and compliant. As the two of them go off to bed, I lie there contemplating how much more effective they are in these situations than I am, and how psychologically aware. The other day in the park they were climbing a tree with some other children, one of whom pushed the other.

'That boy she pushed was her brother,' Lawrence explained.

'Really?'

'Mm. Sibling rivalry.'

On Saturday evening I run the bath and get out the bath toys. Lawrence is going first. Which toys should I put out? Hmm, there's the somewhat arthritic wind-up fish . . . the headless My Little Pony bubble bath to which Lydia is still fondly attached . . . I settle on two boats, the plastic teapot – which doubles as a handy, low-tech hair rinser – and a Power Ranger.

Just then the phone rings and Lawrence gets it. He's been invited to a disco.

A *disco*?

'Where?'

'The Old Football Club.'

'How much?'

Never mind my child associating with unsuitable characters or how he's going to get home afterwards, how much are we in for?

'Ten pounds.'

'Ten *pounds*?!'

A bit steep, considering it doesn't include any tequila slammers.

'It includes drinks and *glow sticks*,' he says, evidently frustrated by my relentless interrogation, i.e. two questions. All right, three.

It suddenly occurs to me that we're potentially on the brink of a major developmental milestone here. I must delve, but casually, so as not to seem intense.

'Will there be any girls?'

'*Girls?*'

You'd think I've asked will there be smallpox.

'Everything isn't about *girls*, Mummy. The idea is to have some drinks and a good time!'

He puts his head on one side, widening his eyes to emphasize how witless I am. He thinks I don't get this, but I do. He's in that interim phase when he's interested in going out, nothing more. So this occasion may yet be a milestone, not just because it'll be his first grown-up-style social event, but because it marks that peaceful period in his life before he starts trying to measure up to what the opposite sex might expect. And sex is still viewed as both disgusting and tedious, valid only as a topic for jokes. We know he had enough of it in Year Five to put him off for life.

Later, when the children are asleep – or meant to be – we go in and turn out their lights. Lydia is knitting, sewing and Nintendo-ing in a nest of wool and paper, and Lawrence is absorbed in a book on how to draw dragons.

We go into the bathroom, and Peter gestures at the side of the bath.

'Look,' he says.

The boats, plastic teapot and Power Ranger are exactly where I left them, dry and unplayed-with.

'Aaaah!' I say. 'The End of an Era.'

'I know. We can start clearing out this drawer.'

I breathe on the steamed-up mirror.

'Oh, look . . .'

Fragments of their past drawings reappear, like happy ghosts.

'We haven't seen those for ages . . . What?'

Peter has gone quite misty-eyed.

'It's just all going by so fast.'

Not this again.

'Come on, let's clear out this drawer. You know how you like to do that.'

And we start putting the boats, Power Ranger, headless My Little Pony bubble bath and arthritic wind-up fish in a bag.

'But what if they haven't totally finished with them? What if they want to play with them again? For old times' sake.'

'You're right. Let's just throw out the broken ones and put the rest back in here.'

'We can check with them in the morning.'

'Yeah.'

We just need some time to adjust.

Another way to tell what stage children are at is by their virtual vocabulary.

Any mention of 'puffles', the round fluffy-looking pets in *Club Penguin*, and you know they're between five and eight. After that it's Tom Nook and red turnips: *Animal Crossing*, age seven to ten. And now we have cool, urban eleven- and twelve-year-olds dashing away from the television muttering,

'Sorry, Mum: have to go and harvest my rice.'

When other boys rush upstairs after school to play *Call of Duty* or *Battlefield*, with their Realistic Warfare Scenarios, Lawrence joins his sister on *Farmville*, where the most extreme event is a cygnet turning into a swan.

It's brought out a side of the children, particularly Lydia, that's so far remained dormant. The biggest surprise has been not the appeal of ploughing and planting against raking insurgents with machine-gun fire, but going downstairs at 6.45 a.m. to make the tea – as Peter generally does – to find Lawrence already there.

'Hi Dad! I'm just picking my raspberries,' he chirps, tapping away.

The various crops on their farms appear onscreen a set number of hours after they've 'sown the seeds', with a few clicks of the mouse. Looking at the rain coming down outside, I can see it beats real gardening in one obvious respect. But the deadlines are ridiculously precise; on Sunday, after I spent two hours trying to persuade everyone to go to the park, Lydia announced that she couldn't possibly leave the house at that time as her onions were due.

She's now to be found up and dressed on school-days by 7 a.m., way earlier than usual. Meanwhile, the actual pansies I got her for a window box wither unregarded. Naturally I haven't told my mother, whose allotment the children never quite bonded with as she hoped.

'They don't seem to like the chard.'

'No one likes chard.'

And my attempts to interest them in the Real Vegetable Project are faring no better this year than last. If anything, it's worse, because the real things don't even have novelty on their side.

Neither of them took more than a cursory turn with the trowel last summer when Katarina and I put in carrots, two kinds of beans, tomatoes, potatoes and strawberries. I was taken aback by the fierceness of my attachment; I wasn't very good at bonding with Lawrence and Lydia in the early days but I really adored the courgettes. I kept breaking off other activities to rush upstairs and gaze at their gorgeous burgeoning greenness, retie the beans to their poles and check the anti-carrot-fly fleece hadn't blown off. It was like having an affair, only without the hotel bills and guilt.

'And with real tomatoes,' I tell Lawrence, 'you get something you can eat!'

I don't mention that the courgettes suddenly stopped growing for no apparent reason and the carrots only made it to about an inch.

'It's not really about that,' he explains, with exaggerated patience.

'What is it about, then?'

'It's the satisfaction when the crops come up, you know, like when you finish a crossword.'

I'm flattered but *don't* know, as I've never managed it. I once got stuck on an RS homework word search in which the longest word was 'miracle'.

'OK, but with real vegetables not only do you get actual *food*; this all just does seem a bit too easy. Surely the crops are at least prone to being blighted by pests or dug up by rabbits? I mean, you know, where are the challenges?'

'It's not about challenges,' he says. 'It's about having fun.'

He looks at me with the hint of a smile.

'Fun: you remember that, Mummy.'

Just about, I think, when he's gone: *just about*.

Shortly after this, he comes running into the kitchen.

'It's finally happened!'

'What has?'

'Lydia and I both want to use the phone at the same time!'

Knowing that I'm on the lookout for signs of puberty, he looks up at me knowingly.

I was expecting something more along the lines of a cracked voice and hairy nooks. And excited as we are by all this change, Peter and I are currently mourning those vestiges of childhood like the bath toys, or Lawrence's cuddly animals, which are even now being demoted onto the floor of his room.

And I'm still hoping that Lydia will wear the dresses we chose together – 'that you *made* me choose, Mummy' – two summers ago. But I'm losing track of what size she is, because it keeps changing. I can't seem to grasp that she's growing.

In September I got her some jeans. The 9–10s all looked huge, so I got Age 8 and was then amazed when they didn't fit. I was like the out-of-touch relative gasping, 'Ooh! Haven't you grown!' only I live here. Katarina had to take her out to get the right size, plus she threw in a new skirt, leggings, top and beret, in which she looked fabulous – but about fifteen.

I could never have predicted that mere pieces of cloth could cause such appalling trouble.

It started with Peter's sister's wedding. Then we had Diane's. Then there was the *tankini*. The top was actually quite long, and the strip of visible midriff only minimal, so after a hot, exhausting wrangle in Debenhams, I gave in.

Now, it's:

'Why can't I wear a crop top?'

'Because they're tarty.'

'They're not!'

'They *ARE*.'

She is still ten.

'Why did you *buy* it for me then?'

'It wasn't a crop top when I bloody *bought* it! It was a *normal vest*! You *GREW*!!'

'Well, why can't I *wear* it, then?'

'It – is – *TARTY*!'

'I'm *afraid*,' she says coolly, 'I know more about Modern Things than *you*.'

'I don't care. You can wear it to bed, that's all.'

'Going at this rate, I probably am going to hate you as I get older,' she says matter-of-factly, as she leaves the room.

In the morning she gets ready for school and among the PE kit and other essentials I see a pair of sunglasses.

'What d'you need those for? The sun's not even out.'

She perches them fetchingly on her head, giving me a coy look.

'OK, you can wear them for today,' I say.

I'm playing the long game, giving way on the shades so I can keep the crop top at bay for a couple more years. Or possibly months. Time's not behaving as it used to. The days are getting somehow shorter and things speed up, then slow down again. Sometimes the kids wake up seemingly having grown about a year overnight. One morning after a recent sleepover she came home slathered in eye shadow and looking like Jodie Foster in *Taxi Driver*.

A few days later, she says:

'I know it's a long way off, but when we go shopping for my first bra, don't embarrass me.'

An outbreak of bra-buying is currently under way in her class, causing those who haven't yet got one to feel they're – well, behind the curve.

I smart a bit at this, as I pride myself on being rather good at this stuff.

'Well, weirdly enough, I wasn't planning to embarrass you,' I say. 'And in any case you don't have to take me along at all, though it would be nice.'

I look away, trying not to sound as if I'm emotionally invested. 'How would I embarrass you, anyway?'

'You know, by holding it across my chest in the shop and saying loudly: "*Oh no, you'll need a C!*"'

'Because that is so my style.'

She looks a bit deflated.

Careful now . . .

'How awful,' I add. 'Who on earth *would* say that?'

'Miss H. She told us in PSHE.'

Even my mother managed to perform that ritual without humiliating me in public, and she used to sing in the street. Actually, she was pretty good at the delicate stuff. She never criticized the Biba 'Midnight' eye shadow I began wearing at thirteen. And even before that, at the first sign of Hair in an Embarrassing Place – i.e. my face – she went to the chemist for the pungent ammonia and hydrogen peroxide to bleach my upper lip, while I hid behind the blinds, wondering if I was turning into a werewolf. I was still at primary school.

The first time their body mutinies, in whatever way, is a milestone but one that it's easy to overlook or dismiss. I must make sure to follow my mother's example – I don't say *that* very often – and not belittle any of Lydia's concerns. It's so easy to say: 'Don't be silly! Of course you don't look fat/ugly/weird/short/like an alien,' and make them furious. One must tread carefully.

'So,' I say, 'if you are going to buy a bra, of course I'll come with you. If you want.'

'I know! You just said that!'

'Er, well, I don't know. You might want to go with your friends. Or get it online.'

'Why would I do that? I'm obviously going to need to try it on.'

'Of course.'

'There is one thing, though.'

Brace yourself.

'I probably will need to get *two*. So I can put one in the wash and wear one.'

'Good idea!'

It seems my financial prudence is finally rubbing off. And I don't say:

It would be an even better idea if when one is dirty you put it in the machine and do the actual washing rather than leave it lying on the floor, which I bet you will.

'I remember my first training bra,' I say. 'Though why were they called "training bras"? Training them to do what?'

'Ha! Of course I want you to come with me. So stop worrying about it, OK?'

'I'm not.'

'All right, Mummy. Whatever you say.'

Then the tables are turned.

I buy myself a new top that I hope should place me safely in the respectable-but-not-entirely-sexless middle ground between Ageing Slapper on Budget Hen Night and Regional Manager of Executive Parking Designation Invited to Take Early Retirement. I've also bought a small wheelie case.

Last year Lydia's lot went on a school trip and she was the only one whose bag was wheel-less. Is disabled luggage now a Thing?

'I had to *carry* it!'

'For God's sake, listen to yourself. When I was young, we had to stuff every piece of clothing we owned into a huge plastic bag and drag it to the *launderette*. You don't even know what that *is*.'

'*And* you went up the chimney and down the mines at the same time,' says Lydia, exchanging a smirk with Lawrence.

'Oh, ha ha. Well, I've got you a wheelie case now, so you can be nice to me for a change.'

It's actually for me as well, but I don't say this. Instead I put on my new top and admire it in the mirror while she unwraps the case. A sticker on the side says '*Expandable by up to 20%*'. She bends down, peels it off and before you can say 'tits up', has stuck it to my chest.

Peter and Lawrence laugh their heads off.

'Right,' I say, twisting away so she can't grab it back. 'I'll wear it to take you to school.'

Credit Crunches

'Two girls at St Bollocks are pregnant,' says Lawrence.

'Don't be ridiculous. Who told you that?'

After a guilty pause:

'Jack.'

'Mr Reliable.'

'Yeah! Me and Tom counted how many lies he told today.'

'How many?'

'Forty-three. Huge ones!'

Our children never lie.

Except . . .

Though it's hard to believe – looking at that round, innocent face – it appears there has been some, as Hillary Clinton would put it, mis-speaking about a detention.

'I'm putting you in charge of that,' says Peter, his way of sliding out of anything he doesn't want to do.

And it matters, because it's vital we establish mutual

trust now. He's given up the bath toys, gone to his first disco and begun borrowing my phone.

There's no time to lose.

Except it's not fair to make *me* deal with this. I have no powers of deception, whereas Peter is *so* convincing I sometimes overhear him lying on the phone and am completely taken in. If he gets a cold caller trying to sell him anything, he's quite capable of saying he can't talk just at the moment because he's on his way out to hospital with a tumour, and I find myself thinking: 'Shit – are you?' If Lawrence has learned to dissemble from anyone, it's his father – not me.

Also, as someone who's never learned to prepare what I'm going to say before I say it, I'm at a further disadvantage. In my family you had to grab the chance to speak whenever there was a gap, whether you had something relevant to say or not. And my formative years were heavily influenced by a youth improvisation class in which we were always just given the first line and had to make the rest up. So I just start talking, and hope it will magically come together by the end.

This time, though, I try doing the same as when I'm abroad: formulate a statement in my head first to see if it makes sense. To my surprise, it's not bad out loud either: compassionate but morally unequivocal.

'I saw the detention in your home book,' I tell him.

'You know, you *can* lie to me. And I may not even find out. But our relationship will be far better in the long run if you don't.'

Yep, I'm really pleased with the way I've put this; I think I'll put another Effectiveness badge on my fleece.

'Look, Mum,' he says. 'There's the new Renault!'

And I look round.

It's not just the sense of being outmanoeuvred that's unsettling, but the discovery of yet another stage of juvenile development I seem not to know about. I mean, we lied to *our* parents, obviously, we had to – but my little Lawrence? And he's years away from operating at full strength.

Peter points out that he hasn't actually *lied*, just not told us.

'He's trying out Need to Know,' he says. 'I mean, a few years from now he's not going to be telling us everything he's done on a night out, is he? So he's – you know, limbering up.'

'Yeah, well thanks for your help.'

'Did you tell *your* parents everything?'

'Just – go away.'

Though I hate agreeing with him, I wonder if this is indeed a kind of resourcefulness that will stand the lad in good stead.

A child with guile is less likely to be taken advantage

of; it's vital as part of the even more essential life skill of Questioning Authority. In the event of being told to stay at their desks while a plane was crashing into their office block, or to wait in a burning building, would they ignore it and run for their lives?

This matters because, let's be realistic, they're going to need to mistrust the powers that be. Well, we all should, all the time, but especially now.

The economy's in trouble and why? Because the banks have been Not Telling Us Stuff, big time. Several have collapsed. Confidence in the financial system, in credit itself, has plummeted. And while that doesn't sound entirely bad, it could get much worse. By the time they're old enough to earn a living, we could be at the end of the financial system as we know it.

So the very least I can do is try to explain this to them, even though I don't understand it. It's just that Peter understands it even less.

'How could the banks have been giving out money they hadn't even *got*?' says Lydia, dismayed to discover that fairy tales and the real world aren't in fact separate as I've always claimed.

'Exactly,' I say. 'I have no idea.'

What I do know is that our holiday this year – assuming we dare go on it – will cost 30 per cent more than before.

'You used to have to hand over only 67p to get a euro,' I say. 'Whereas now it'll cost you almost £1.'

She is horrified.

'And – that Coke that was two euros, a few years ago cost £1.34. Last year it was £1.70, and now it'll cost us £1.96.'

'*WHY*?!'

'Er . . . because money goes up and down. It's . . .'

Luckily she loses interest at that point and runs off.

And we too have done some editing of the facts, for we are facing our own credit crunch. Peter has cast off the yoke of salaried employment – or rather, it has cast him off – and we are now both self-employed. As Oscar Wilde so nearly said, to have one freelance writer in the house may be regarded as amusing; two really is careless. We have told the children there will be less money coming in, but have at no point used the words 'running', 'out' or 'of'.

There's frankly never a good time to become self-employed. Lawrence needs new shoes and is starting to hang over the sides of the chair we got him from IKEA to go with the cabin bed when he was about six. I've already given him my old desk, and my father's drawing board is behind the dirty washing box, ready and waiting for whoever becomes an artist – because one of them is bound to, right?

'You do realize they'll probably be doing all their drawing on screens by then?' says Peter unhelpfully. 'If any.'

And he tells *me* not to be negative.

I also know, from a tip my mother gave me, how to see off the perpetrators of store cards and other extortionate forms of credit:

'I'm afraid I don't have a regular income.'

They whip those forms away before you can say, 'That'll be 29 per cent – a *month*, you sucker.'

And it will soon be Christmas.

We're being bombarded with catalogues of useless accessories from companies who have bought our address in the deluded belief that we have any spare money. The most optimistic of these, a well-known candle and scent brand, invites us this Christmas to 'define his boundaries' in study, car or den with something called a 'Scent Surround Cube' costing – how *can* it? – £95.

'My boundaries are defined already,' says Peter, 'with a uniquely invigorating mix of compost, sock and bin.'

He's always been keen on recycling and reusing, and has recently discovered Freecycle, leading to visits from women in multicoloured knitted Peruvian hats who come and remove our unwanted electronic goods.

'See?' he says. 'I can still get attention from other females.'

'I'm going out to forage,' I say. 'Try not to give away my computer.'

Remembering the 'distressed' kitchen stools we once picked up there, I go to the dump and return with a fake leather and chrome office chair for Lawrence.

'Kids,' I say, 'Look at this. It was just sitting there – completely free!'

They are in awe.

Lawrence and Peter set to work on it with the Jif, and soon his room takes on the ambience of a small advertising agency, albeit one in which visitors are also greeted by several damp towels and an ominously overflowing bin.

Next, I turn my attention to the state of his lace-ups. With a 5p-sized hole in each sole, he can identify different species of leaf on the pavement without looking. I wondered why his socks were coming back wet.

'But it's OK, Mummy,' he adds. 'I could use my birthday money to buy some new ones.'

I feel terrible; I've overdone the 'money doesn't grow on trees' dissertations and turned into my father. At least he had the justification of having been poor.

'No, you don't have to do that,' I say. 'I'll get you

some new shoes, but you'll have to save up for the luxuries, the way I used to.'

'I know! You told me *a million times*.'

I've been trying to establish this habit since well before the financial crisis. It resulted in the single bout of car-washing last summer and a recent, one-off session of leaf-raking, leading me to wonder if he regards paid labour the same way he saw nursery after his first day, as a novelty you experience only once.

At least he knows how to save. Whereas he lovingly tends his cash, taking it out of its box regularly as one would exercise a pet, Lydia is only fleetingly intimate with hers. She spends her pocket money on the day – if not before – and is absolutely a product of the shallow, consumerist society that is now being shown up for what it is: shallow and consumerist. Her room is littered with ponies and assorted other species, each member of which – at the moment of purchase – she believes will ensure lasting happiness. And lately, when we watch TV, she has taken to calling out names of the products in the ads like a competitor in a particularly unnerving pub quiz.

'*Fragrances the whole room . . .*' says a smooth voice.

'Ambi-Pur!' shouts Lydia, followed by a sideways glance at me. 'I know, Mummy: "fragrance" is not a verb.'

Last night in the bath, when I brought in some tangerine slices, she looked up at me and said:

'Why not enjoy the Christmassy taste of orange?'

And, when I gave her an apple after supper recently, she said not 'Yum!' or even, 'You have the rest,' but:

'Join the AA.'

So on the one hand her brain has indeed been completely infiltrated by advertising. On the other hand, it was gratifying to see the extent to which Britain's leading motorists' organization had so comprehensively failed to reach its target.

Still, she is only eight years away from her first credit card – if they still have them by then, and now, in the midst of the debt crisis, I'm already imagining her as one of its victims.

'I'd already got four hundred handbags and two thousand My Little Ponies,' I can hear her confessing on *You and Yours*. 'I'd even lost my home. But the bank kept encouraging me to take out more loans.'

She wants a junior potter's wheel for Christmas and is leaving nothing to chance. There is only one in the shop and it might get sold to someone else. At 7 a.m. one day I come in to wake her up to be confronted by a piece of A4.

'It's a map of the toy shop, Mummy! So you know where to go.'

The shop is about a hundred metres from our house. And the junior potter's wheel – and the till – are clearly marked with giant arrows. And to ensure the absent-minded parental brain doesn't get confused on the way out like one of those poor satnav victims, the door is labelled 'Door'.

So we buy it, and she plays with it once, and I continue my increasingly desperate efforts to imbue her with the joys of deferred gratification:

'If you save it up you'll have *more*, see?' – which have so far come to naught.

However, by focusing as usual on the negative I have underestimated her brother. One afternoon he lays aside his Geography homework and in his smart new shoes, fixes her with a sympathetic yet firm look, like a very small doctor.

'Lydia, look: if you save £20 I will give you five.'

'Five pounds? That's a lot,' I say. 'It's – er, 25 per cent.'

'I'm *trying* to teach her to save.'

Her eyes light up at the thought of a fiver but she's less clear on the method by which to achieve it. He, by contrast, has accumulated £60.

'How did you get so much?'

My mind flashes back to Lydia's school Open Day, when he discovered a worrying talent for shove ha'penny. And I recently found a gaming chip in his bedroom which he claimed was a novelty bookmark.

'By *saving*, obviously. See, Lydia? You could have this much if you just don't keep spending it.'

He's right; if she would only curb her addiction to small fluffy animals. But the savings–interest concept eludes her.

'Mm, will I really get £5?' she murmurs dreamily, and before her brother or I can explain the terms of the deal, in her mind she has already got the fiver and is leaping to her feet to go and spend it on a purse filled with tiny plastic horses. Just then, their father comes in.

'Who wants to wash the car with me?'

'Me!'

'*Me!*'

They've been promised £2 each, and when Peter reports to me at suppertime, I get a surprise.

'Lydia actually did the most.'

The connection between effort and reward finally established, she flops down with her chammy leather, glowing with pride.

The following morning I find Lawrence on the landing doing sit-ups.

'Hey, Mum. Come and join me!'

I lie down beside him and lift my head towards

my knees slowly and not at all smoothly, like a DVD on picture search. The last time I visited a gym I was childless and could still bend all the way into a squat without getting stuck and falling sideways like a crashed robot.

'Good, Mummy!'

I have a pain in my middle as if I've had an organ removed without anaesthetic, but there is a glimmer of achievement.

'I should really do this every day,' I say.

'You can. I'll be your personal trainer!'

'Tell you what,' I say. 'I'll pay you 20p a go. I need a chart with boxes to tick, though. That's the only thing that works with me.'

'Cool.'

When I next come downstairs, he has made an A4 chart labelled *Coach: Lawrence, Student: Mummy*,' with boxes to tick for each day of the week.

'And,' he adds brightly, 'if you attend all the sessions in the week, you get one free.'

When my willpower evaporates and it's clear that Week One will be the *only* week, he takes to following me round the house babbling, 'Gissa job: I can do that,' like Yosser Hughes in *Boys from the Blackstuff*, Alan Bleasdale's bleak 1982 drama about the destruction of a Merseyside community through unemployment resulting from the demise of its traditional industries. Though he lacks the intense, manic desperation – and three children – that put Yosser up there with the great tragic heroes, he does share his ill-fated tendency to set himself challenges he isn't quite up to, in his case cleaning all the windows in the house before *Top Gear*.

The following day he sets his sights more realistically on the bin drawer, a deadly cavern encrusted with the spatterings of a thousand dinners, which Peter and I thought a brilliant idea when we first saw it in a friend's house, the same as my parents did with venetian blinds in the sixties, never thinking it would one day have to be cleaned.

'Are you sure?' I say. 'You have to lift out the bin, the old bread tin with the compost, *and* the huge drawer.'

To my surprise, he is straight in there, like David Attenborough in the infamous bat cave, as the fumes from the droppings overwhelmed him and his final words were audible only as a croak.

When he emerges, the drawer *and* the alcove are spotless; we are still averting our eyes, though now from the dazzle of its whiteness. I hand over a fiver. But Lydia is feeling left out.

'Lawrence will have £65 and I won't have anything!'

'He's been *saving*.'

Her understanding of the relationship between not spending money and still having it later is still embryonic.

'Well, think of a job you'd like to do.'

She is low on motivation. Having the guinea pigs to muck out has given her a perspective on cleaning which has rather pushed it down the running as a possible career.

'I have to do it every week and I don't even get any money.'

'Well,' I say, 'that's what comes of wanting guinea pigs; it's like being a parent.'

'There's ice cream for after supper!' says Peter, sounding like the persistently cheery wife in *The Truman Show*.

'I don't want ice cream,' says Lydia. 'Can I have money instead?'

'No,' we both say together.

'Why not? When I got a toy at the airport, you let Lawrence have the money.'

'It doesn't apply to food,' I say wearily, 'because otherwise . . .'

I lack the will to go on.

Eventually we wave them bedwards and slump down in front of the TV. About ten minutes in, Lydia appears with a small piece of paper.

'*Head Massages and Hair Fiddles,*' it says. '*Only 10p a minute.*'

'Very good. We're up for that,' we say. 'But tomorrow. It's bedtime now.'

Then Lawrence comes down with a larger sheet, advertising foot rubs at the same rate but with a discount for regulars. Also, his ad has a Before and After, with the After foot going '*Mmm!*'

'He's copying me!'

This sparks a turf war, which only ceases when Peter and I both agree to get into bed early and be manipulated. Lawrence does the feet and Lydia the heads. It's wonderful.

'Put yourselves to bed; we'll pay you tomorrow,' I murmur.

'We don't give credit,' is the last thing I hear as I drift away.

The Art of the Deal (2)

The lovely woman who looked after my sister and me as children used to admonish us gently from time to time for being *unladylike*. She was much stricter than both our parents about manners and endeavoured to stamp out troglodytic habits like grabbing toys from each other or eating with our mouths open, which we generally got from Dad.

Yet I am by far the *less* ladylike of the two adults in the house. In the early days of our relationship, Peter was practically traumatized when I once ate a lettuce leaf straight from the salad bowl. It's taken him more than twenty years to tame me to an acceptable level, though I'm still given to road rage, shouting at the television and swearing vigorously at the squirrels currently vandalizing our bird feeders. That the children regularly shout 'Bugger off!' at them while banging the back door is entirely thanks to me.

As a reward for being particularly good at the moment, I have bought them a large bottle of a well-known carbonated soft drink. They have quite a bit of it at supper, and are soon exchanging burps like an end of the pier novelty act from the days before comedy was funny. The burping's bad enough, but Lawrence embellishes it with an imitation of a boy at his school who is a proficient burper, complete with actions.

'He pushes his chair back at the same moment, see? And then it looks as though the force of the burp has propelled him backwards!'

'Something,' I say, 'that only eleven-year-old boys are likely to find appealing.'

Lydia is offended.

'Well, I'm a ten-year-old girl and I find it appealing, thank you very much!'

Until now I've always assumed a fascination with bodily expulsions to be a predominantly male preoccupation, shared by females only in the very early years. With girls, farts and bottom anecdotes are generally replaced quite early on by ponies, Hannah Montana and chatting to each other on their DSs while sitting next to each other on the same chair. Yet at ten Lydia likes both.

Could it be because she's the second child after a boy? We brought them up on *Thomas the Tank Engine*, *Fireman Sam*, *The Beano* and *The Simpsons* – I vainly hoped she'd take *Lisa* as a role model – though I suppose there was also *Top Gear*.

We built endless towers of Lego for them to knock down. And when we inherited Peter's nephews' toy cars, plus a garage with ramp and wind-up lift, I suppose a male-ish slant was established as the default. She never really took to my old dolls' house and it was Lawrence who tucked up his cuddly toy animals at night, including the 'twins', Tortoise and Elephant: 'They're both eight.'

But why should playing with toy cars lead onto expelling air at the supper table? And Lawrence was never a *boysy* boy in any case. As well as being devoted to the animals, he has never played a violent computer game. Well, not in this house. And when we visited a family with two girls, he was far more fascinated by their toy supermarket than Lydia was.

Maybe we should just follow the fashion and blame it on their viewing habits. The obvious culprit is *A Knight's Tale*, a medieval variation on *My Fair Lady* starring Heath Ledger as William Thatcher, a peasant who fakes it as a knight. Near the end, almost like an outtake, the main characters have a farting contest, where the loser – whoever's farts are the quietest – has to buy a round. And the pretty female blacksmith holds her end up, as it were, with the men. Just possibly,

Lydia has remembered that scene better than any of the stuff about chivalry, or even Paul Bettany naked. Yes, I think it must be that.

But although the burping is tedious, I prefer my daughter this way. She is never coy or mimsy and knows herself to be her brother's equal. And if that means she occasionally sounds like a halfback on a stag night, we can probably live with that.

Shortly after this, the kitchen sink stops emptying properly, and without a murmur of protest Peter gets his rubber gloves on and goes outside to unblock the drain. He is soon joined by Lawrence, who also grapples personfully with the stinking sludge as, inevitably, it starts to rain. I look up from my biscuit dough and over at Lydia, who is stitching a top for her toy rabbit. I'm pleasantly surprised by how quickly Lawrence jumps to it.

'I guess clearing the drain really is a boy thing,' I say.

'Definitely a boy thing,' she says.

'Look at you,' I say when he comes back in, 'elbow deep in the slime while Lydia sews. I guess as a male you're programmed to do that stuff.'

'Don't be dumb,' he snorts: 'Dad said you'd give me a pound.'

The Eternal Wisdom of Sid Arthur

Saturday afternoon. Lydia has lots of homework, and I have a pile of admin. We discuss which order to do our tasks in. Then we get some chocolate mini rolls, curl up on the sofa and watch *Total Wipeout*, in which people run along large inflatable things and fall off them into water.

Later, a schoolfriend of hers comes over and happens to tell us about Sid Arthur, who gave up striving for understanding, sat under a tree to meditate, gained enlightenment and gave the world Buddhism.

It's a pity Sid Arthur never wrote a parenting manual. You just know that people who would never watch *Total Wipeout* and eat mini rolls with their kids would probably do it if some expert said it would help get them into Oxbridge.

I'm against too much striving in children, particularly when it involves having to drive them anywhere or enforce any kind of extra-curricular regime such as music practice, especially at weekends, when most

Stephanie Calman

normal people are in bed with a hangover. We know they *will* learn to feed themselves, get on a bus without falling under it and eventually even become adults. But for some reason our generation is unable to let them do this; our children have to be endlessly chivvied, cajoled, pushed, tweaked and *fixed*. It's like adding six teaspoons of baking powder to a cake because it just has to be better than one.

My mother has always cited the precedents of world-class high achievers who frequently slipped their brains into neutral, where inspiration flowed more freely. James Watson and Francis Crick famously stumbled on the structure of DNA while consorting with girls and playing tennis – well, if not literally in bed or on the court, at least not hunched over a microscope twenty-four hours a day, while their parents muttered: 'Must . . . Win . . . Nobel Prize . . .' And others were working on it too, taking the pressure off a bit.

And Winston Churchill of course won the war – and wrote fifteen books – while drinking a pint of champagne a day plus several whiskies, bricklaying, and painting landscapes. Plus he often worked in bed *and* held meetings while he was in the bath.

But none of them would match up to the exigent standards of the Modern Parent.

I didn't always think this way. I used to be hard-working and miserable. I didn't take holidays and believed that the tiniest treat had to be earned, even having the radio on while I did the ironing. Then I had children and discovered Fatigue.

Once you've woken up on the floor a few times with a one- and a two-year-old crawling over you like ticks on a buffalo, you're less inclined to punish yourself any further. And in any case, you prove your worth by doing the really simple things: feeding a hungry baby, kissing a grazed knee – and yelling, 'For the last time, will you all *SHUT UP*!!' during a sleepover.

But in practice I don't get to relax with the children that often, since being married to Mr Marvellous has pushed me into the role of Enforcer. Because of his refusal to be the bad guy I have no choice but to wield the big stick on things like teeth brushing and, yes, homework. And it's even worse when, like a shadow chancellor, he makes wild promises he thinks he'll never have to keep, such as signing a contract agreeing to buy Lydia, for her fifteenth birthday, an alpaca.

Katarina, who grew up in Slovakia, tried to reason with her:

'My aunty had to get up at 4.30 a.m. to feed the pigs, you know.'

'Don't,' I say, though she's right. It's just that these reminiscences usually make anyone frustrated with the English education system sigh with envy; under the Communists they did Maths every day *and* treated their elders with respect.

'Don't worry,' says Peter. 'It's five years away so she'll have changed her mind by then.'

He obviously doesn't understand children and their long memories. Decades after my father took me to Paris, my sister – who'd been left behind because she was too small – was still reminding him regularly of his obligation:

'How's school?'

'Fine. Don't forget you still owe me a trip to Paris.'

So don't come crying to me when you're scraping alpaca poo off the carpet. On balance, though, you could say that my enforcing role makes these off-duty moments all the lovelier.

When Peter comes in with a bundle of work under his arm to find us still in front of the TV, the guilt rises in me.

Then Lydia says:

'We're creatively recharging.'

And I know that Crick, Watson, Churchill and Sid Arthur would approve.

Freedom Riders

Lawrence is off to his friend Alex's house, to stay the night and – we hope – see *X-Men Origins: Wolverine*, so we don't have to. Alex's mother has offered to take them, but in the event she does something way more useful, which is to instigate Lawrence's first adult-free bus ride.

We live in a part of London only patchily served by public transport, a bit like the Empty Quarter of the Arabian Peninsula, so even parents with better things to do find themselves spending about a third of their waking hours in the car.

But all that is about to change; our son has now received his age 11–15 Oyster card, giving him free bus travel. It sits by his bed at night, shiny with the promise of unaccompanied future journeys, although it could potentially bode ill for fitness. A neighbour's child is so smitten with hers she now takes the bus to the sweet shop, one stop away. However, Alex's house, like so many destinations only a mile or two away from here, requires at least two trains or buses. So I drop him there.

But today is definitely The Day.

He returns the next morning, looking unusually happy.

'How was *Wolverine*?'

'Fine. Shall I tell you about our journey home? Alex's mum told us to get the 258 but it didn't go from that stop so we took the 227 instead and found our way from there!'

This is major. Not only has he taken his first bus ride without us, he has had to use his Initiative, one of those parts of the modern child you feel sure has withered through disuse and become pointless, like the appendix.

'And,' he adds, 'we gave up our seats for old people.'

I tell my friend Lucy, Milo's mother.

'Good,' she says, 'because Milo thinks we should let them go up to town together.'

'Town as in *town*,' I say, 'with all those thieves and weirdos?'

But Milo is an old hand. He has to get several forms of transport across the suburbs to school every day, and has really matured; he's now about forty in travel years. He reads the paper on the train and has opinions on everything. Maybe it's convinced his parents that he isn't twelve at all, but an adult in a slightly crumpled blazer. Is she perhaps overestimating his capabilities?

'Hm. Where in town?'

'Oxford Street.'

'With the huge crowds, hustlers and pickpockets? *That* Oxford Street?'

'I know, I know,' she says. 'But it's OK because I thought we could shadow them. Possibly in disguise.'

'What, in burkas?'

This is too absurd, even for me. On the plus side, it makes her sound far more anxious than me. My strategy is to promise freedom at every opportunity while not bestowing too much – a kind of post-9/11, New Labour parenting.

'They wouldn't see us. Well, Milo wouldn't.'

'Lawrence certainly wouldn't; he can't see a dark sock on a pale carpet.'

Mind you, nor can anyone in this family. The whole place looks like the doorway of a charity shop.

Every week – every day – brings some new crisis of lost pen, protractor, gym shorts, trainers, library book or tights. This morning, when the stress levels were already at maximum, neither of them had their PE kit. 8 a.m. and we were all flinging open cupboards, yelling at each other. I could feel my life expectancy plummeting. If I wanted to spend my life looking for other people's clothes I'd be a PA to a celebrity and get paid for it. At 4 p.m. they came out and – guess what? Both PE kits had been at school *all along*. I'd wasted all that energy shouting which I could have used for something else.

How will they get anywhere in life with this inability to think ahead? Barack Obama didn't get where he is today by forgetting his kit.

'I was going to run for president, but I lost my speech.'

Or other top leaders. Can you imagine Julius Caesar saying to his mother:

'I've got to invade Britannia, but I can't find my armour.'

'Well, where did you invade last?'

In the end, Lawrence and Milo go to town, look round the music shops at the various guitars, and come home safely.

Amazing.

The next day, Peter and I are in town and instead of going home to collect them, arrange to meet our two at the local cinema. They get the bus there from home without a hitch; we have an argument and get off at the wrong tube stop.

'You have to remember that Clapham has three

different stops,' Lawrence explains when we arrive, growling and late. 'You should have got off at the Common.'

'I know! He made us get off at the wrong one.'

'Now, now,' he says. 'Stop it or Lydia and I will go home.'

'Unlike him,' I say, 'I'm from London. I never get these things wrong.'

'Shut up now: no one cares.'

Lydia hasn't yet widened her horizons by exploring the possibilities of the transport network. I know the best way to stimulate interest is to withdraw the private taxi service, but whenever I imagine her walking up a badly lit street – such as ours – after getting off the bus or train, I lose my nerve. And Peter's worse. What she does want though, and right away, is a phone.

She starts following me round the house asking for one – occasionally bumping into Lawrence, who is already shadowing me with the same aim.

'Hey, you're like those little aliens who follow Buzz Lightyear around in *Toy Story*,' I say.

'That's not funny, Mummy.'

In my day, the first stages of maturity were: getting your own front door key, learning how to 'French kiss' – how incredibly pre-European that sounds now

Stephanie Calman

– and starting to smoke. There were some who managed it all on the same day. A classmate of my sister's even had a specific sequence for getting off with boys, of which one was 'Kiss on the Cheek' and five – the last one – 'Kissing in Vest and Pants'.

Now quite a few milestones seem to be signified by the acquisition of branded objects. There are one or two really well-off kids at Lawrence's school whose – shall we say . . . *values*? – may I fear be undermining our simple way of life.

'We can't be going skiing every five minutes and driving to school in a Porsche Cayman,' I say. The children have skied once, in Slovakia with Katarina, where it costs £5 a day for everything. Our car is the same age as Lydia, and when it was last put up on the ramp for its MOT, the mechanic winced.

'I *know*,' says Lawrence. 'I don't *care*. Can I just have a phone? And it's *Cayenne*.'

'The Cayman is actually the hard-top version of the Boxster,' adds Peter.

'Whatever,' I say. 'I was joking, anyway.'

And anyhow, who wants a car named after a notorious penal colony? You don't see the Ford Devil's Island, or the Vauxhall Siberia.

But what you do notice is that everyone, rich or otherwise, nowadays seems to want more *things*.

146

Privately, I'm leaning towards giving way on the phones, but when mobiles first came in, and were not yet ubiquitous, I made a bet with a guy I used to work with that I'd wait until the kids were fourteen, and I don't want to seem weak. Mind you, I said I wasn't going to get married, have children or move to South London, so any credibility I once had has evaporated.

In the end I decide to deploy Peter's customary strategy and promise we'll return to the subject in depth, just as soon as I can really focus on it. I can't help envying the government, who can play for time on all sorts of problems, knowing they're bound to be voted out before it all catches up with them. When Peter doesn't want to do something, he says, in a vaguely positive way:

'It's a thought.'

So you go away believing it's being considered.

Or you do if you're not married to him.

Ages 11 & 12: The Third Parent

Whereas Lydia isn't visibly changing yet and is still able to revel unselfconsciously in her alt persona of forest sprite, her brother has been to a paintballing party and come back with a moustache. He's not quite twelve.

Since I'm fairly sure he didn't have one yesterday, I'm assuming a mixture of dirt and paint has blown onto his upper lip. I've been using that excuse myself since about 1974.

Still, even if technically not a real moustache, it immediately has an effect on his behaviour.

'Have you done your homework?' he asks Lydia sternly.

'He-llo?' I say. 'Peter, did you know there's a third parent in this family?'

'He's known for ages,' says Lawrence.

Peter, disloyally, laughs.

Come to think of it, this is not an entirely new phase. He once told Lydia:

'If you don't play sensibly, I'll throw you in your cot.'

She was two: he was three and a bit.

'I *have* to do most of the parenting,' Lawrence continues, 'since you don't do it.'

'I *do* do it, except when you won't let me! Now shove off and leave your sister alone.'

When he does, I notice he now has the beginnings of shoulders and a fashionable, shuffling walk.

It's this contact with the outside world. You send them off to a birthday party, in this case a simulated gun battle, and they return that bit harder, more confident. And frankly more obstinate. Where I grew up, there were kids who lived mostly outside, from the age of about six. They had homes and families; their mums just didn't like them messing the place up. My mother came across one of them one evening sitting shivering on the kerb, and asked why he didn't go home. He said:

'Can't: I'm not allowed back in till ten.'

Then you had the other extreme, the ones whose mums didn't want them mixing with the first lot. Their faces remained soft and their dinner money was to be had easily, right into middle age.

We go out to lunch, and afterwards Lawrence says:

'Did you notice?'

'What?'

'They didn't offer me the Children's Menu!'

Later, when we all gather round to argue about whose turn it is to lay the table, Peter says:

'Nobody warns you how brief their childhood is going to be.'

'Yes they do,' I say. 'They warned us constantly. Pretty much the whole time from when they were born, people have said to us: "Watch out: it goes by so fast."'

At the weekend, Lawrence calls up the stairs:

'Lunch is ready, Lydia! Come on, I won't tell you again!'

Not this again.

'Hello? Going on at Lydia is my job.'

It appears that as he approaches his twelfth birthday, our older child has not only *not* moved on from his Third Parent phase but is seeking to widen the distance between him and childhood, as repre-sented by his hardly much younger sister. Maybe it's also the result of encouraging them to watch the film version of *Freaky Friday*, though I don't know how they took it in, as apparently I ruined it by inter-rupting.

'I'm just saying it's a copy of a much earlier book, *Vice Versa*,' I pointed out, 'which is about a father and son swapping lives and was written ages ago.' (1882, would you believe.)

'Whatever. Just shut up, OK?'

'And I like Jamie Lee Curtis, but this really isn't very good.'

'It isn't with you talking all the way through it!'

Vice Versa itself has been adapted many, many times, and you can see why the theme of adult–child role reversal has never lost its appeal. Who doesn't occasionally want to escape from their prescribed persona, each trapped in their own mould of the social bun tin, to enjoy the freedoms and privileges of the other side?

Of course, when you're a child you don't think: 'Isn't it nice not having to worry about bills and mortgages and tax, and all the things that manage to be simultaneously incredibly stressful *and* incredibly dull?'

You just demand more control over your life without the faintest idea what's coming down the pipe.

When the children introduced the swear jar – the one that helped fund their first games consoles – they were quite little. I know because of the different prices for each word, and how Lydia spelled *Bluddy* and *Bolax* on the chart she made. At one point Lawrence had a go, you know, just to test out the words. And without even thinking I found myself automatically becoming the child:

'So *you're* allowed to swear,' I said.

'Yeah.'

'That's so unfair!'

Bluddy bolax.

You actually do see that in life sometimes, in families where the parents are scared of responsibility and continually ask the children what they should do – which is bad; letting the ruled decide things for themselves leads to a breakdown in the natural order, as the Chinese government will readily confirm.

You won't catch us allowing democracy to seep in round here – yet. But it is lurking. We're not helping ourselves, of course, with our weak performances in the leading roles. Peter avoids confrontation wherever possible and when I try to sound authoritative I'm often unconvincing.

'If you don't eat your fishcakes, you'll be in big, fat trouble!' I blustered at supper the other night.

At which, not surprisingly, both children burst out laughing.

And suddenly I didn't care whether they finished their dinner or not because I was so grateful for a moment's respite from the awful burden of anxiety that I'm always criticizing in others but am totally in the grip of myself. I realized, with a jolt, that I operate quite a lot of the time in just two fun-free modes: worrying about them, and telling them off.

If I could have an alternative role I wouldn't choose Child, but Divorced Dad, so I could stop nagging them to brush their teeth and do their homework, and get to be the Fun One, taking them go-karting, bungee-jumping and to McDonald's every weekend – because all the boring stuff would be their mother's job.

'Hey kids, Peter's away! Let's watch four DVDs! Let's live on crisps!'

Who doesn't want to be the Popular One?

Maybe the next few years will bring some opportunities.

'Hi, I'd like to apply to be the Popular One.'

'And your kids are . . .?'

'Um, coming up to twelve and thirteen.'

'HAH!'

Trespassers Will Be Irritated

After a couple of months' exhaustive negotiations Peter and I have given way, and both children now have a thick lock of hair hanging over one eye known as a 'sweep', i.e. a fringe that leans to one side as if pulled by an unseen string, which is the last word in cool coiffure. It is the Look, as it were, sweeping the nation.

Lydia's morning ritual is now 20 per cent brushing her hair and 80 per cent staring into the mirror to see if it's moved. And a forcefield has materialized around her which repels the slightest parental touch. When I lean across to put a bit back in place, she springs back as if I'm wielding a machete.

'Leave my hair alone!'

'But you've got a bit falling forward. I just want to . . .'

'Leave it! You've got no sense of – hair.'

'I do,' I plead feebly. 'I have hair.'

'Well, you've got no sense of *my* hair.'

She gives me a warning glare.

The other night I was reading to her – for the first time in ages. It's such a rarity now, I was trying to make it a quality experience for us both. But she was far more absorbed by her hair, whipping it this way and that.

'Can you stop flicking your hair around?' I said.

'Why?'

'It's distracting. You can't listen and do that at the same time.'

'I can multitask.'

I waited for the ironic smile, but she kept a straight face.

Lawrence is a bit less combative, though equally preoccupied. The first time I smoothed the dreaded sweep back from his forehead, he batted my hand away. And his latest habit is to fall silent or even vanish in mid-conversation as he rushes to the mirror to push a stray strand into place. Even table tennis – the sport you can play without running – takes twice as long as it used to because he has to stop between each point to put back his hair.

So the hair on both our children is now off limits, like an expanse of countryside closed off by the Ministry of Defence. All I can do is gaze wistfully through the wire, remembering the days when their father and I roamed free among them, brushing and smoothing their golden curls and never imagining they would become so incredibly *bossy*.

After supper I tell Peter:

'I'm just worn out with being pushed away all the time.'

And he says,

'I know, me too. Hey – he's asleep; let's go and move his hair.'

The hairdresser takes her position on the front line of this battle in her stride, waiting patiently, scissors poised, as we go tiresomely back and forth:

'A bit more off the back and sides than before I think.'

'You're joking! Last time I was practically shaved!!'

Shaved is his term for anything off at all. By his standards James May is shaved.

'Well fine,' I say. 'You look like you're wearing a Terry Wogan wig.'

'Who even *is* that?'

All he needs is a frilly shirt and he could present a 1970s variety show. That, and a new catchphrase, instead of:

'You make me do *everything* and never let me do *anything*.'

'It's all part of the development of their autonomy,' says my mother. 'The moment a baby first realizes it's a separate being from its mother is the first stage on this journey . . .'

'Yes,' I say.

'When it seeks the breast, and it isn't presented immediately—'

'Mm, I know.'

She has her own version of multiple personality disorder, where they're all therapists. Except she isn't one.

'Then when it grabs the food out of your hand . . .' I say.

'Oh, yes.'

'To throw it all over the room . . .'

'Ha, yes! I remember you saying, "Me do it!"'

She does this in her weird baby voice that I find unsettling, with a sort of scrunched newborn face that I can tell she is also doing, even down the phone.

'Then they start pushing away the spit-dotted tissue when you try to wipe their face at the school gate.'

Back on safe ground, phew.

And now this with the hair.

When he was about three, I once referred to him as 'my lovely Lawrence.' And he said:

'I'm not *your* Lawrence. I'm *my* Lawrence.'

Come to think of it, *that* was probably the first sign of adolescence.

Too Clever by 0.5

I recently met a woman who said she doesn't want her children to be cleverer than she is. It certainly made a refreshing change to find someone actively *not* trying to get their kids into the best school, Oxbridge and whatever comes after that – world domination, or possibly a bottomless void full of giant serpents as on an ancient map. But it was also a bit weird.

What's she afraid of? You *want* them to outshine you, don't you? My dad said he longed to be asked one day, 'Are you Stephanie Calman's father?' and ideally not by a truancy officer.

I do want them to outshine me – but maybe not *quite* so relentlessly as they are starting to now.

I get what is probably my last opportunity to tell Lawrence something he doesn't know, in a cafe, while we're ordering our drinks. As we wait, we notice the latest kind of absurd novelty water on display. This one says on the label in large letters *'This Water'* and underneath, in smaller type: *'is made from water and clouds'*.

'Water and clouds?! Do me a favour,' I say. 'Look on the back. I bet you it's got sugar in it.'

It has. My poor twelve-year-old is disillusioned.

'Do you have to crush my world?' he says.

Of course, he wasn't that *illusioned* in the first place. Following a life-changing moment while watching a Channel 4 documentary about the sandwich business, he has been disturbingly well informed about the hidden evils of processed food, snatching ketchup bottles from the chubby clutches of small children and exclaiming:

'Twenty-eight per cent sugar: that's nearly as much as Fanta!' until they whimper for their mothers. And when I came in the other morning, opened the fridge and said to him, 'You've eaten the last piece of bacon,' he said, 'I am the future: I deserve the bacon.'

Having had no further education I'm totally used to not being the cleverest person in the room, so it's not hard for the children to get the better of me. And since Lawrence demonstrates his superior intellect with a knowingness which can be amusing, I try just to sit back and surrender. For example, when I told him the other morning that I had a big lump behind my ear, he said:

'Yes, that would be your head.'

I imagine this is what it would have been like to

have had a really annoying older brother. On the plus side, it did dispel the brain-tumour-leading-swiftly-to-premature-death scenario I had been dwelling on.

His sister is more direct.

When I tell Lydia, who's messing about with her food, to Eat Properly, she answers:

'Tell me *why*, using five adjectives and two synonyms.'

To be fair, this is partly her reaction to the campaign by the education system to ruin children's writing with swirls of lexical garnish. You know the kind of thing: *I nervously entered the dark, mysterious wood, and looked up anxiously at the tall, old, brown, wooden trees . . .* You'll pass the exam, but it'll take years to clear away enough of the textual silt to be able to write a sentence that you – or anyone else – might enjoy. Reading English essays these days you have to be like the Princess and the Pea, trying to detect the tiny nuggets of meaning beneath all the layers of padding.

At weekends she sits in front of the television, aiming her vast reserves of scepticism at the cosmetics companies and exposing their venal motives by jeering when those deeply cleansing *fractalides* and complex chains of *polybibbles* come on to flog yet another shampoo:

'"Because you're worth it"?!' she barks. 'If you're *worth it*, how come you need all this expensive crap on your hair?'

We did tell them at an early age about the science behind commercials, i.e. that there almost always isn't any.

She did a homework not long ago – God knows what subject – which was a letter from Rapunzel to a hairspray manufacturer, complaining that their product had caused her hair to break and the Prince, who was climbing up it, to fall down. I think she was going to take them to court.

People complain about children being taken in by advertising before they can talk, but I think this generation is way more sophisticated than we were.

When Peter and I go to see the film of Lynn Barber's *An Education*, we're taken aback to be reminded of such innocent times. Not only does poor Jenny not guess that her suave new lover is married, her parents don't either. And it being 1961, and a true story, they really didn't.

'Imagine trying that on with Lydia,' I say. 'After five minutes she'd have him bang to rights: "Why haven't we been to your house? You've obviously got a wife, *duh*!" And that would be the end of that.'

'Thank God,' says Peter, who doesn't want her to get a boyfriend, like, ever.

She has only just turned eleven, but takes no crap from boys.

And she and her brother are displaying strategic abilities I've never had or even aspired to.

'Six o'clock,' I said, the other night. 'Time for *The Simpsons*.'

'But I still haven't finished my homework.'

'You've done enough,' I said. 'Get to the television.'

'Hah! I did reverse psychology on you!'

And if I'd actually paid attention I'd have observed that she only *appeared* to have worked solidly since coming back from school, doing one part work to about four parts making toast, twirling a hairband round her pencil, glueing some ribbon onto her music folder, checking the weekend magazines for pictures of Lady Gaga and *gazing*.

I say this generation is more knowing, yet I think we find it harder to envisage them as capable adults than our parents and grandparents did with us.

When I was thirteen I got a weekend job as a waitress in a country tea room owned by two spinster sisters. I said I was nearly fifteen – I looked it – and for a Saturday job in a village, no one checked. The other girls were fifteen, out of school and working full-time; counting my tips with them produced the heady thrill of being among the grown-ups. So, after learning how to kiss and smoke, the big leap in maturity was getting a job. By eighteen I'd had several; most of us had.

And this now seems quite rare.

So lately I've been plagued by a new worry: what will happen when the children leave home? What will they study? Where will they live? How will they get jobs? And will they remember to lock the door when they go out? Jessica Mitford didn't know you had to pay for electricity, but at least her excuse was that she was posh.

It's hard to believe they'll ever be capable of these things, because I find I can only really imagine them at the stage they're at now. When they were babies, we couldn't imagine them walking; when they began walking we couldn't imagine them talking; and when they began talking we couldn't imagine them saying:

'Whatever. Can we go now?'

The sort of anxiety that's begun to creep up on us – even on Perfect Peter at times – is now increasingly the norm. Here we are, our children well fed and dressed, with books and toys – not to mention gadgets – and yet we exist, many of us, in a state of low-level panic.

It does seem that those who survived the Depression and one or even both wars were less prone to unwarranted anxieties. When you've glimpsed the shadow of the Nazi jackboot looming over the Channel, you might not feel compelled to drive your child two blocks to a friend's house, never mind watch over them on the slide in case they shoot off the end and scrape their knee. And if you've seen two or three empty seats in the classroom at the start of every school year, as my mother did in the thirties, you're probably less convinced by anti-bacterial wipes.

Those of us born between the late fifties and early sixties were the first to grow up vaccinated against the major killer diseases, the biggest gift to British children since the 1870 Education Act invented the primary school. So you'd think we'd be chilled and even quite thrilled.

But instead of revelling in our good fortune at living in this place and time, we're plagued by fears. What if our children cross the road and get run over? Make a cup of tea and spill boiling water on themselves? Walk to a friend's and get robbed – or worse? Better take them, guard them, do it for them. And if someone's horrible to them at school? Mean online? We feel every sneer, shove and lack of likes as if it were happening to us – even more so.

We're hardwired to protect them, so it's easy to forget that they're continuously in the process of detaching from the mothership, and that our role is to facilitate that. When you make bread you knead it, then leave it to rise. But now, we believe that if we're not constantly *doing* something – with them, to them or for them – we're not parenting. The closest we get to Benign Neglect is letting them learn only two musical instruments instead of three.

I recently read about a woman who discovered her son was having sex at fifteen, a calamity that had befallen him because – she was convinced – he *didn't have enough hobbies.*

There's no time to lose! We absolutely *must* get them to start becoming more independent.

'We must get them to start becoming more independent,' I tell Peter.

'You're right.'

Compared with us at that age, they have it incredibly cushy. Thanks to their father's weak-mindedness, they're still, for instance, being brought glasses of water and so forth at supper.

And if I say:

'Let them get their own!'

He says:

'Well, I'm already at the sink.'

It makes me want to scream.

'You won't catch me doing that,' I scoff, as I set off for school with PE kit, knitting and various other things Lydia's left behind, because I pathetically want her to love me even more than she does already.

So I'm just as bad as him.

But we must *try*.

'Lawrence can do the supper once a week – nothing too ambitious – and Lydia can start making her own packed lunches.'

'Good idea.'

'And stop picking up after them all the time.'

'Absolutely,' he says, putting away their shoes.

In his 1964 novel *A Mother's Kisses*, Bruce Jay Friedman describes the hero's agony as his mother bursts into his first college lecture, having flown from New York to the Midwest to bring him a sweater.

Nowadays, that wouldn't qualify as satire.

At half-term Lydia goes to spend a few days in Wales with her friend Georgie and her family. Peter takes her to Paddington Station, and describes that bittersweet moment when they disappear into the stream of people.

'She sort of floated away,' he said, 'like a little paper boat on the sea.'

'They look so vulnerable.'

So when they turn round to snap at you, it helps.

'Yeah! She knew I was waiting, so told me to shove off.'

When she comes back I offer to collect her, because although she's just travelled a hundred and sixty miles across south-west England, she's never come home on this route across London before. And I know that she *can* find her way, and *will* survive changing to the wrong train at Baker Street if it happens, but I go anyway, because I want to.

I find the last parking space in 'Paddington Bear Quarter' or whatever preposterous name they've now given that area, cut through the hospital loading bay and walk up to the barrier. There's no sign of her. Don't tell me she's missed the bloody train . . .

I wait.

Then I text.

Then I see a young woman coming towards me in the crowd who looks like Lydia, but older, more self-possessed. She looks like Lydia in the future.

Show her you've seen her but don't wave.

I venture a minimal smile.

And she smiles back.

It's as if she exists in the outside world now, rather than in ours.

A Mermaid on Speed

We're on holiday in Grenada.

It's over thirty degrees, too hot to go on a walk to see the waterfalls in the interior – or anywhere much. So we read and swim until dusk, then go to The Owl, a little bar by the beach, where apparently they have crab racing.

The crabs are named after luminaries such as King, Obama, Kennedy – and, um, Brown: Gordon, we assume. As they weave their way slowly across the floor, we pick one each and make bets of one or two East Caribbean dollars, about 40p or 80p. We all cheer on our crabs – even some young Americans from the medical school, who otherwise don't appear to mix much. A little light gambling in a bar is the ideal activity for pre-teens and they will remember it as a highlight of the trip.

The next day we're meant to go snorkelling, but Lawrence and Peter are feeling a bit overcooked. Lydia's already had quite a scary bout of sunstroke, when we had to call a doctor and cover her in damp towels. So they stay put, leaving me – the only one who's really not good on boats – to go with her.

There are about ten other people on the trip. I don't know what I imagined, but the boat is quite small and terrifyingly fast. While the other passengers pretend not to notice, I clutch the side, whimpering, in a stomach-clenching replay of the Madeiran cable car ride when I forgot I was scared of heights. That time, Lydia sweetly did her best to reassure me that it was quite safe, while the two Germans sitting opposite explained how normal it was to be suspended hundreds of feet above a motorway in a tiny glass box. This time, she immediately leaves my side to go and sit right up at the front, leaning into the spray like a gleaming figurehead.

We drop anchor in the middle of the sea. Everyone else gets their masks on and steps confidently off the side, including Lydia – who shoots across the open water like a mermaid on speed, while I get in still holding the hand of the boat guy, who to make it worse is disconcertingly handsome. Twenty years ago I wouldn't have had to worry about the snorkelling. Now I'm just an anxious white tourist old enough to be his mother.

'That's my daughter!' I tell him as she whizzes past, followed by: 'I don't think I can do this.'

'Sure you can,' he says.

At least she isn't hanging around worrying about me; that feels like an achievement. My family were *so* unathletic, we did no sport or games and neither of my parents ever learned to swim; to be in the middle of the Caribbean, watching my own child moving through it like a seal, is beyond imagining.

I eventually let go of the poor guy's hand, put my masked face in and see the coral and amazing coloured fish. I've done it! When we get back to land, Lydia is aglow – we both are.

And I realize that though I would have been disappointed in myself had I not managed it, we're reaching the point where Lydia is increasingly surpassing me – not difficult in the water – and that's how it's meant to be.

It's not my place any more to dazzle: it's hers. And every time I recall the sight of her charging across the ocean, I feel incredibly happy.

It's not just pride but also relief, that we've produced a physically confident child who takes life on her own terms. I don't have to keep proving myself any more, or beating myself up for being crap at tennis, or never having tried skiing, or failing the audition for the nativity play choir after singing flat in front of the whole school. None of it matters any more.

'So basically,' says Peter, 'you're going to start living through the children.'

'Yeah! It feels great!'

The thing about mermaids, of course, is that they never stay on land for good.

Postgate and Firmin's Stars

Many middle-class parents worry about the pernicious influence of the media on the developing minds of their offspring, something we gave up on years ago.

Lydia is currently addicted to *My Super Sweet Sixteen*, about the ludicrously extravagant birthday celebrations of rich American teenagers, and *True Beauty*, in which model types compete to show that they are also Beautiful Inside. I manage to stick about four minutes of it, during which the contestants have to try to display sympathy when one of them gets chocolate on her gold shoes.

Her generation is being indoctrinated all right, to aim for fame by television. Luckily she has so far resisted the lure of *The X-Factor* and co., but then things take a worrying turn.

She is widely praised for her dryly humorous portrayal of Polly the Maid in the end of year school play, *The Rocky Monster Show*. A couple of other parents stop us in the car park. Then the drama teacher utters the words every self-employed parent dreads:

'She could be an actor.'

At the age of eleven I joined my friend Tilly at a drama group – and not just *any* drama group, but the one run by the legendary Anna Scher. By fourteen I was going on auditions, rushing out of the house with the light in my eyes and no idea that I hadn't a chance in hell. Not only are they a truly brutal assault on the self-esteem, you almost never get the part. Most actors are unemployed for most of the time, some for pretty much their whole lives.

There's only one thing for it.

I make her sit through *A Chorus Line*, the film of the hit show which caused a sensation thirty years ago with the revelation that every high-kicking row of nobodies who dreamed of stardom was a mass of heart-rending internal struggles – and some were even gay.

In the middle of it, Peter comes in and says:

'On behalf of my generation, I'd like to apologize for the hair in this film,' and goes out again.

Sadly the hair is the most dramatic thing in it. Seen in the harsh light of 2010 sensibilities, the story is now quite dreary – as a non-dancer Michael Douglas had to play the choreographer sitting down – and Lydia utterly fails to get the message.

'Why did you like this film again?' she says, before drifting away to her knitting.

Luckily there is another hit from the past whose themes of insecure minorities and group survival versus individual self-expression have withstood the temporal tides. It's also far stronger on both character development and narrative tension: *The Clangers*.

We start with the BBC4 documentary I have hitherto failed to persuade her to watch, about Oliver Postgate and Peter Firmin, who created the show. In it they explain how they built the sets, did the sounds, and even customized the camera. They made the armatures out of Meccano, which intrigues her as Peter still has his entire set upstairs.

We are already fans of *Ivor the Engine*, their leftist social vision as seen through the lives of an eccentric Welsh community and their stubborn yet loyal train, but *The Clangers* has somehow slipped past me.

'I always just thought it was a bunch of faintly irritating characters who make a stupid whistling noise,' I say in my defence.

'Well, it obviously isn't!'

We immediately order the box-set, which Lydia devours with a dedication and concentration rarely seen in an academic setting.

For the rest of the holidays she is never without

her needles, a ball of pink wool and a downloaded picture of Tiny Clanger, all of which come with us wherever we go, but eschews Peter's offer of exclusive access to his Meccano. He keeps the hundreds of narrow metal struts stored in the compact but shockingly heavy chest of drawers his father made for it in the sixties, when the evenings stretched out endlessly in the Time Before YouTube.

'Actually, I'm going to use pipe-cleaners.'

Then I discover there's an exhibition of models and drawings from British animation on at the Cartoon Museum. I design the outing genuinely as a holiday diversion, not a career nudge. But I can't resist nurturing a tiny hope that This Could Be It. And Peter Firmin himself is giving a talk! This must be Fate.

I make sure we get seats in the front row, and afterwards tell the great man we're among his biggest fans.

'Lydia – show him Tiny Clanger. She's made her own Tiny Clanger.'

Firmin takes the little replica and examines the embroidered red panels of the felt jacket.

'This is good,' he says. 'Did you download the BBC pattern?'

'What pattern?'

As soon as we reach home it's clear – to me anyway – that for Lydia, immortality will be achieved not through speech, song or dance but wool.

What a relief. We're looking forward to a future with no twisted ankles or backstage histrionics, no tears and slammed doors after yet another unsuccessful audition – no shouting 'It should have been me!' at the live transmission of the Oscars; just peaceful clicking and the occasional '*Tch*' after a dropped stitch. That, and a house coated with fluff.

To paraphrase Oscar Wilde, we are all in the gutter – but some of us are looking up at Postgate and Firmin's stars.

Superpowers

When the kids were small, I couldn't get them off to nursery fast enough. Weekends were exhausting, and the holidays a dreaded expanse of blank time. When Katarina started she could only do two days a week, and I looked forward to Tuesdays and Fridays with a terrible desperation.

Now I stop work eagerly at ten to four, so I can hear their jokes and witness every nuance of their thrilling journey through life. Hooray for school! When I don't see them for eight hours a day I love them so much more.

I even look forward to helping with their homework. Or them letting me pretend that I am.

'Would you like to help me with my Latin?' Lawrence says kindly, even though the nearest I get to helping is gazing vaguely at a word like *navis* and saying,

'Is it something to do with ships?'

'Good, Mum!'

He's been trying to teach me to say: '*The man is*

telling the people who are coming into the city to go out again.'

It's just a question of finding the right moment to say it – possibly if I open the door to someone from UKIP.

I didn't pay much attention at school after the age of about fourteen, so knowledge-wise, the only way is up. I remember nothing from Physics except making a little weighing scale out of a straw to weigh a Smartie and Lucy burning part of her eyebrows off in one of the few experiments we actually carried out, instead of using the stopclocks to play *Just a Minute*: 'Kate: you have sixty seconds to talk about – lip gloss.' And wasn't 'Mini, midi, maxi' what Julius Caesar said? I spent History, which focused mainly on the Unification of Italy, dozing peacefully at my desk – though by the look of it, so did quite a lot of Italians.

So with Lawrence I feel a warm glow. I'm no longer a middle-aged woman marooned on the intellectual hard shoulder but his pal, discussing declensions before we go and make a stir-fry together for supper – OK, actually made by me. I even volunteer for those agonizing sequences of almost-but-not-quite-identical shapes known as Non-Verbal Reasoning that Lydia occasionally brings home, as if we're in an Obama-style campaign with a slogan like 'Together We *Really* Can!'

This is SO GREAT.

'I don't know if I ever want them to leave,' I say. 'In fact, I know I don't.'

To my surprise, Peter – the normal one – feels the same.

'Maybe what we need to do,' he says, 'is start focusing on the times when they're really badly behaved, and concentrate on those. That should make it easier.'

Right!

Those of our friends with full-blown teenagers are definitely eager to see them move on. The children of the British middle classes are criss-crossing India, Africa and beyond – teaching, building schools, losing their passports and just being Out There. One is even cycling up – and I suppose down – the Andes; his parents seem thrilled.

But how do we train ourselves to feel the same?

Peter's friend Philip, who has four – so only himself to blame – says that if he takes fifteen-year-old Sophie and her friends anywhere in the car, he is ordered not to speak.

'What, at all?'

'At all.'

So he's quite looking forward to her going off.

And his friend James's daughter, when she used to ask for lifts at that age, would say:

'Thanks Dad – what will you be wearing?'

Mark, whose daughter went to boarding school, says he was told:

'OK, when you arrive, go through the gates and *stay in the car*. Also, don't wear those dreadful shorts.'

'How were you supposed to attend the event if you weren't allowed out of the car?' I ask.

He shrugs. 'Await further instructions I suppose.'

In my day, the grown-ups assessed *our* appearance, not the other way round. Though my father sometimes had holes in his jumpers and my mother once came to collect me in a maxi-length blue and gold kaftan, it would never have crossed my mind to criticize their wardrobe. However shambolic they were, you just didn't.

Other friends ahead of us on this path warn of financial and domestic devastation. Ah, well *that* should definitely make us less keen.

We must prepare ourselves for nights interrupted by the front door banging as they come in at all hours, trails of dirty clothes along the landing and hordes of their mates descending on the place like locusts as soon as we go out. But we won't dare protest, because then they'll drift away and expose themselves to drugs, alcopops and Pot Noodles.

'But we love our children; we don't *want* them to leave.'

'Ah, they'll soon turn into monsters, just you wait.'

'And in any case,' says another, 'they don't leave for ever.'

Philip and Emma's two eldest are now at university, and they're considering moving house.

'Downsizing? Makes sense, I suppose.'

'Actually, no . . .'

They're getting an even bigger place for when they all come back.

But before we have to worry about any of that, we're coming to the next milestone, and the End of an Era. Well, where we see an ending, for him it's a beginning. From September we will no longer be walking Lawrence to school.

We've been on notice for about a year, as more and more of his friends have begun to walk or take the bus. And it's pretty much our only exercise: half an hour at a brisk pace past the chestnut trees, with a three-metre sprint in the middle to avoid getting flattened on the South Circular, a terrifying speedway with a crossing island about the size of a lilo between you and certain death. It holds only about four people in intimate proximity, and if one of you reaches out to adjust your bag or even scratch, whoever's at the edge is flipped into the road.

So there's that.

Also, he's not yet demonstrating the level of maturity I'm looking for. Along with drinking black coffee and filling the bathroom with the smell of synthetic cedarwood and manly Lynx top notes, he's taken to sauntering across the road without looking properly, like Jean-Paul Belmondo going up the Champs Elysées in *A Bout de Souffle* – though one of the reasons JPB looked so cool, I suspect, was that he didn't have his mother running after him shouting:

'You didn't look both ways! There'll be no *Simpsons* tonight!'

And Paris's most famous thoroughfare has nothing on the South Circular.

To be fair, he *is* growing up and would be utterly feeble if he didn't try to push his luck a bit now and then. As Peter says with tedious regularity:

'My mother told me not to ride my bike beyond the end of the road, but I didn't get where I am today by doing what she said.'

He does *not*, however, say this to Lawrence.

It's left to me, as usual, to state the obvious and absorb the ensuing flak.

'I *am* looking,' says Lawrence. 'You just *assume* I'm not.'

He may well be right on this, but I don't like to

give ground. I have in my head a maternal satnav which doesn't intone '*Turn left*' or '*Turn right*' but '*Look out!*' and '*Aaargh!*' in a panicky squeal.

I consider suggesting he *shows* me he's looking by very clearly turning his head, the way my driving instructor taught me to do for mirror-signal-manoeuvre, so the examiner couldn't miss it. I can just hear the exchange at the school gate:

'Oi, Lawrence. Why do you do that weird nodding thing when you cross the road?'

'Oh, it's quite normal: just to show my mum I'm looking both ways.'

Then I step out from behind a tree.

Aside from that, it's such a nice walk we sometimes argue over whose turn it is. There are two parents and only five days in the week, so it's never fair.

The new school is so near he'll almost be able to leap from his bedroom window through the gate. And what we adults will miss, apart from the exercise and the chance to get all the conkers before everyone else, is the conversation.

It used to be fairly basic topics, like which country the sick stain on the landing looks like – most of us think China – to topics you might call a bit more sophisticated.

'Say you've got a square or a hexagon.'

'OK.'

'And all its sides are equal. You can turn it six times, or four if it's a square, so that it fits into itself. So the Order of Rotational Symmetry is six.'

'Great!'

I try to think when I can use this in everyday life: 'We've just bought a table for the garden.'

'Ah, but what's its Order of Rotational Symmetry?'

Sometimes he tells me the names of clouds. I tend to get cumulo-nimbus mixed up with nimbo-cumulus, for example, so he often has to tell me again. Or he explains about unstable compounds, which makes me think of marriage, one reason he's likely to go to university whereas I never did.

Or sometimes we just walk along designing our ideal house. We're both quite keen on energy-saving features, like a magnetic force that could suck all the rubbish into a chute straight to the dump, or a device to prevent unnecessary bending. Or we choose which superpower we'd like to have. I've once sat in front of a whole chocolate cake and not eaten it, but I don't imagine that counts.

'Right, Mummy: would you be able to fly, become invisible, be telekinetic or set things on fire?'

'I'd choose telekinesis.'

But my reason is totally sad: to make shirts iron

out their own creases and used games kit leap up the stairs. That's the trouble with parenthood. It not only reorders your priorities to the point where you go into a lingerie department and automatically look for something with ducks on it, but even re-edits your fantasies. I *should* be saying I'd like to be able to fly over the Grand Canyon or to Mars, but I wonder where I'd put my alarm clock and change of pants. One of my dreams at his age was to be able to get into a sweet shop at night without being discovered; now it's wanting socks to jump into the dirty washing box. At least at twelve I had some ambition.

Occasionally I think of something *I* know, like:

'Do you know why Goldfinger's number plate is AU 1?'

And he says,

'Yes. It's the symbol for gold. You've told me that, like, loads of times.'

'Oh. Have I?'

So I suppose that was the last autumn I will ever walk home for breakfast, my pockets bulging with conkers like advanced ovarian cysts, and the last time we've stood on the bridge and waved at the Eurostar zooming along beneath. Gone are the days when we stopped to watch a digger. And perhaps last Friday was also the last night I will ever wake up, boiling hot, an unexpectedly smooth, slender arm flung over my face and a sharp little knee in my side. How many Lasts are we going through, without even realizing? But – looking on the bright side, maybe soon we'll no longer have to say,

'Go to *bed*! Daddy and I are trying to have what's left of our evening!'

To which Lawrence now retorts:

'Don't have kids, then!'

We have now arrived at school. I gaze up at the chestnut trees, taking a last look. He was three when we first brought him here, carrying his Duplo crane to show the Head.

I ask him:

'Are you looking forward to being older?'

'Yes. I want to learn responsibility.'

I want to ask whether this could start with finding his pencil case, PE bag and swimming kit, all currently missing. But just the thought of saying it again is *so* tedious I say instead:

'What are you looking forward to most?'

And I am not at all prepared for his answer.

'Driving. And getting a girlfriend.'

So we've gone from superpowers to *actual* powers; adulthood is no longer some mythical state, but clearly visible on the horizon.

'Really? I thought boys of your age viewed girls as – well, pointless.'

'No way! Mum . . .' He grips me by the arm. 'You have NO IDEA.'

'Eh?' I say, 'What d'you mean . . .?'

But the bell is going.

'Never mind,' he says. 'Let's think of somewhere to walk to when we no longer have to walk to school.'

'Mm, that's a nice thought,' I say, wanting to savour the moment. But he calls 'Bye!' and goes through the gate, leaving me completely disoriented, like a swimmer flipped over by a sudden change in the current.

Doctor Not in the House

The Jewish American comic Rita Rudner used to tell a joke about a pregnant woman who says to her friend:

'We've had the scan and we know what it is: it's a lawyer.'

And we're now pretty sure, eleven years in, that we've had a doctor.

Lydia has announced her intention to Do Medicine. Top Trumps! If only my father was alive; ideally you need at least one Jewish or Asian grandparent to fully experience a moment like this. It's our reward for not being overly ambitious.

'See?' I want to say to all the pushy ones, with the Oxbridge Entrance questions pinned to the sides of their cots: just be laid back and chilled like us, and your children will be effortlessly brilliant.

It starts with *Doctor in the House* coming on TV.

It's decades since I've seen it, and I'm surprised to find it doesn't contain that much actual doctoring; most of the film is taken up with James Robertson

Justice barking at people and a plot by one St Swithin's rugby team to steal the hospital mascot from the other.

Lydia *loves* it. The medic's life, particularly the flirting and mascot-related subterfuge – with patients a peripheral distraction – hugely appeals.

'You do know that being a doctor isn't mainly hiding behind doors and stealing toy pandas in striped scarves, don't you?' I say.

She fixes me with a furious stare.

'OF COURSE!!'

We tell quite a few people, as having comprehensively failed the sciences both Peter and I are beside ourselves with excitement, but also awe; medicine is properly Grown Up. And she is genuinely keen on doing Biology and Chemistry to GCSE and probably beyond, so it's definitely no flash in the bedpan.

OMG OMG OMG! Our daughter is going to be a *doctor*!

Her weird preoccupations and extreme lack of squeamishness are now starting to make sense.

Handily, I have also just learned of the Wellcome Collection, a world-renowned research body with a huge trove of bizarre and somewhat macabre finds from Henry Wellcome's extensive travels in the nineteenth century, such as shrunken heads – which look like testicles with faces – and antique fertility charms, including a Japanese one of a naked ivory couple entwined inside a tiny hollowed-out gourd. It is *perfect* for kids.

They also hold lavish exhibitions, copious talks and events, all free. Fancy 'A Guided Tour in British Sign Language of the Institute of Sexology', for example? And there's a library where you can look up obscure medical info like the first use of mare's urine in fertility treatment.

'This is such great timing!' I tell Peter. 'This place is *ideal*.'

As Lawrence is also feeling quite *sciencey* at the moment, I take them both, starting with 'Meet the Elements' – a lively, browsing sort of event one Friday evening with a delightfully non-educational ambience, more like a party. The demonstrations include liquid nitrogen being spilled onto a table where it forms tiny droplets that jump around as if they're alive! Wow!

'Because it reaches boiling point below room temperature,' explain the demonstrators.

I am absolutely none the wiser, but the kids look vaguely as if they understand, which is what counts. After all, my role now is purely as the vessel for their greatness. So when I see on the website that Professor Brian Greene – Director of the Center for Theoretical

Physics at Columbia and *literally one of the Cleverest People in the World* – is coming to talk on string theory, I say to Lawrence:

'Let's pop along!'

It doesn't matter that I don't even understand the *title*; all I have to do from now on is *facilitate*. My grandparents escaped an absolute monarchy so that their children, when they had them, would be free. And when my confidence failed me, my dad would say:

'We didn't flee all this way on our flat feet so you could give up,' in a really supportive, encouraging way.

So I now see myself on a continuum, a player in a greater story, The Calman Trajectory, my lack of academic achievement a blessed irrelevance. I doze off in my seat to the erudite murmur of Brian Greene's multiverse, relaxed in the knowledge that my children are going to Do Great Things in the World.

Peter and I then take them back to the Wellcome, to see 'Skin' – a comprehensive exploration of everything from tattoos to the bubonic plague, which holds their attention for *four hours*. Lydia is particularly fascinated by a twenty-minute video on impetigo, featuring abundant close-ups of ravaged arms, torsos and so on, and watches it three times.

That night, she goes to bed with the British Medical

Association A–Z Family Health Encyclopedia (Revised Edition), which has some really juicy pictures.

Soon after, she demands a hefty and quite dense two-volume work on anatomy for her thirteenth birthday.

'It's quite expensive.'

'But it's for her career, so . . .'

'Isn't this exciting?!' we say to each other, about once a day.

Then one day I realize doctoring hasn't been mentioned for a while. The British Medical Association A–Z Family Health Encyclopedia (Revised Edition) is back downstairs and the two-volume work on anatomy sits in a corner of her room, gradually disappearing under a mound of clothes.

Not long after the last sighting of the anatomy books, I come in to a really hideous smell emanating from the kitchen.

'Um, Lyd? What's that on the stove?'

I know she's not interested in cooking.

'A mouse skull. I'm just getting it clean.'

And she busies herself cheerfully with some little bones on the dining table, like Delia Smith at a crime scene.

'And – is that a scalpel?'

'Mm. Got it online.'

'You know what?' I tell Peter. 'I think her thing could be pathology!'

I've just heard Professor Sue Black, the famous forensic anthropologist, on the radio, and I have a feeling about Lydia's speciality, you might say, *in my bones.*

'Hey, Lyd. There's this woman who identifies people who've been dead for ages, hanged from trees or killed in wars and stuff. She went to Kosovo, and – well, anyway. And she identified a paedophile just from the unusual shape of the end of his thumb on the edge of a picture. Amazing, eh!'

Surely this is the closest humans will ever get to having superpowers.

She looks at me blankly.

'Cool. I'm just off to Mimi's to get a mouse – a whole one.'

'OK. And – why?'

'To stuff, of course!'

'Right.'

'They've got a load of them in their freezer. For their pet python.'

She skips off happily down the road.

'I feel we've veered off a bit here,' I tell Peter, my hope of being a doctor or pathologist's mother still glimmering faintly on the mental horizon, now less a vision than a fast evaporating mirage.

'It's good that she has such varied interests,' he says.

When I come down later to make supper I am greeted by an unusual tableau.

Mimi's mouse is standing in a home-made transparent box, holding the little ukulele keyring Lydia got in her Christmas stocking, but with the actual keyring removed so it looks as though it's playing the instrument – like a tiny rodent Eric Clapton.

'Wow,' I say. 'How did you know what to do?'

'YouTube. It's really easy. You just have to make sure you don't pierce the guts, so they don't leak. You have to get the skin off, a bit like pulling off a sock. First you make a shallow cut, at the sternum . . .'

'OK, that's great, thanks.'

'I think I'll do a rabbit next.'

'Don't tell me Mimi's got those in her freezer as well.'

'Of course not: their snake is far too small. I'm going to get one from a reptile food supplier.'

Well, duh.

Then while she's browsing frozen mammals, Peter finds a dead squirrel, lying neatly in our garden, at the edge of the pond. And her eyes light up, like Indiana Jones's when he sees the golden idol.

'What did it die of?'

'It's got no marks or anything: natural causes, I suppose.'

'Can I have it? Please please?'

'Really we should nail it to the back door,' I say, 'as a warning to the others.'

Once you've seen a bird feeder after they've finished with it, you realize these 'cute little creatures' are in fact mindless thugs. They also bite the heads off baby birds. If we'd deployed them to fight the Nazis, the war would have been over much sooner.

She removes the skin, stuffs it, and mounts it on a little podium made from part of a wooden board inscribed 'Hola from Spain' that someone brought back from Barcelona with a gift pack of chorizo. She also gives it a bit of branch to lean against that fell off our largely fruitless pear tree, from which it stares out alertly through new glass eyes. When the tail falls off it's propped up behind it, with – the final touch – a mothball tucked discreetly beneath like a little orange poo.

It immediately becomes our most popular visitor attraction, and, more usefully, distracts us from dwelling on how much we spent on the two-volume book on anatomy.

Ages 12 to 14: *Monsterosa Deliciosa*

So: I've become convinced that adolescence is not a sudden meteor shower but a process that begins in childhood. Still, there are stages. And of those, it's the ones after puberty we find the most challenging, with good reason. In the past there's been great emphasis on bodily changes – hands up if you remember The Curse – but the Modern Parent knows there are issues of far greater import.

The children are far better informed about their bodies than I was, they talk to each other more, menstruation is on the National Curriculum, there is the indispensable PSHE, and everything else – fortunately and unfortunately – is online. Though we don't realize the significance of it yet, Lawrence and Lydia have been born just in time for their first information about sex not to come from porn. Lawrence's school sex video – and that episode of *Friends* – are, in a way, the best things ever to have happened to them on that front.

This leaves us free to worry about all the other stuff. For instance, your child is listening to some music you don't recognize, and you say:

'What the bloody hell is *that*?'

Or, being a Modern Parent, you don't say that, but nod knowingly. Still they can see the blank look in your eyes. And anyway, your liking it slightly spoils it.

Or you come in and they're laughing at something on their phone, and when you ask if you can have a look, quickly close it and say:

'It's not important.'

It's those seemingly smaller changes that can be the most painful, like when they come back from an adventure weekend, or a stay with friends, and you rush to hug them. And they take a step back.

Then there's the extreme self-consciousness you get at this stage; suddenly, everything you say is lame, stupid and wrong, and you just wish you could say the right thing, the cool thing, just *once*.

For your dear, sweet child, so trusting and mild – well, ours never were, but anyway – has gone. And in her place is a genius who knows everything. She is in effect from the future, while you, like the Renaissance Church confronted by Galileo, dwell in the past. You've gone from being the Oracle to the

Village Idiot. If any of this sounds at all *exaggerated*, imagine you're in a Jane Austen story, life going along much as it always has, with the carriages and the whist parties, and fatal attacks of pneumonia caused by wet hems – when in chapter twelve you innocently open a panelled door and find yourself in *Bladerunner*.

Did you ever try to get in with the cool crowd at school and fail? Well, that's about to be your life all over again. And to make it really humiliating, the cool kids are just that – *kids*. Thirty-or-whatever years younger than you. You've got a whole life behind you, with achievements, experience and knowledge; they haven't even taken their GCSEs. But *you* know nothing. Oh, and if you're reading this and thinking, 'Actually, no, this doesn't apply to me: you see I was *in* the cool crowd' – shut up. No one cares.

Terry Wogan – one of the most famous and well-loved broadcasters we've ever had in this country – was once asked in an interview:

'Your children must be very proud to have such a successful dad. What do they say, when you come on?'

And he answered:

'They say, "Not you again!" and switch off.'

This is now your life.

*

Meanwhile, your teenagers want to be appreciated, need desperately to be *praised*, but throw it back in your face. But you must persist. This, I admit, is not easy.

Sample dialogue:

'Is that your Art GCSE project?'

(Mumble)

'It looks really good.'

'What? It's total crap. Anyone can see that!'

In fact, what they mean by 'It's total crap' is actually:

'Thank you, I'm really grateful for the compliment but for reasons that are unclear even to me I am unable to express this.'

One way round this seems to be to copy Michael Caine.

In his famous screen acting masterclass, the star of five decades shows actors how to underplay it. Unlike stage acting, where people in the back row have to be able to see you're sad or scared or angry or whatever, acting on film is minimal.

And transitioning from being the parent of children to the parent of teenagers is much the same. For example, when Lawrence or Lydia came out at home time with a picture, we *used* to say:

'OH WOW! WHAT A LOVELY PICTURE! LET'S

PUT IT RIGHT UP HERE ON THE WALL WHERE
WE CAN ALL SEE IT! HEY EVERYONE, COME
AND LOOK AT *THIS*!'

And they would be very pleased.

Now, when they do something impressive, such as
passing an exam or sewing a top or starting a band,
we must not sound Too Pleased. Nor must we hug
them and cover them with proud, delighted kisses.

'Oh, that's good: well done!' is about right, though
on second thoughts I might lose the '!'.

Similarly, when they say, just as the front door
swings shut:

'I'm off to drift around the streets till I'm sucked
into the maw of the city's swirling, lethal underworld
– bye!' I try to aim for something like:

'OK, see you later.'

Obviously not all teenagers are the same. Ours
will tolerate a smile or pat on the back – may even
welcome it. But some will shrug you off and downplay
their achievement *so* much it sounds as though it's no
achievement – in fact, they're not even in a band at
all; it's another of your pathetic parental fantasies. Or
they *are*, but they're going to give it up because you're
being So Embarrassing.

It's a pretty big adjustment.

I'm terrible at underplaying, so when I do try to

tone it down I often fail, especially if I look at them; Lydia hates being looked at. Like the man in *The Great Escape* who gets caught out by the Gestapo officer saying, 'Good luck', I just can't dissemble. I'd be shaking his hand and saying, 'We're in disguise, isn't it great? Those Nazi fuckers are so thick!' before realizing where I'd gone wrong.

Peter's friends Philip and Emma say it's all about sounding casual. Their four – now in their twenties – were always a bit more amenable when being driven somewhere.

'Eh?'

'Because,' says Peter, 'when you're driving and they're behind you, you're not looking them in the eye.'

'What if they're in the front?'

OK, you're looking at the road, obviously.

'So maybe we should try to create similar conditions.'

'What, sit or stand in front of them and start a conversation, then gaze into a non-existent rear-view mirror, as *if* in the car.'

'Well, sort of.'

Sigh.

I think they simply don't like it when we're too *eager*.

I'm working on reducing my eagerness to an acceptable level when I notice Lydia's reaction to displays of emotion over events that have nothing to do with us, for example in the news.

If it's an abused animal story, I must sympathize – discreetly – but if I gasp at, say, pictures of children who've lost their parents in a tsunami, she hates it.

And I'm just thinking, *how unreasonable* – when I remember I felt exactly the same about *my* mother, abruptly sitting up in her seat and exclaiming, 'Ohhh!' at the TV during the civil war in the Lebanon or when there was another killing in Northern Ireland. Sometimes she'd fling her hand across her mouth, as if in a silent film. It was so *melodramatic*.

So maybe my twelve-year-old's 'bizarre' behaviour suddenly makes a bit more sense.

And today, I have an excellent opportunity to get it right. Well, to *try*.

She's going to the park to meet a boy.

Don't overreact. Don't overreact. Don't overreact.

'Will you be back for lunch?'

'Yes: I'm meeting him from 9 a.m. to 11 a.m.'

'That's very – precise.'

When she comes back, I just about manage to look unbothered. But Lawrence plunges right in.

'How was it?'

And she says:

'Fine.'

And he says:

'What did you do?'

'Nothing. Just chatted.'

'Just chatted? Anything else?'

'No. What would we do?'

'I don't know. What do kids your age do these days?'

He's right: he is the Third Parent after all.

There are several pretty girls in his class, and he's been walking one of them to school. I only know because I happened to glance out of the window at 8.20 a.m. as he was going up the road. Or should I say walking *with*? She's not a poodle.

Don't make a thing of it.

'You may get snapped up by one of them,' I said naively at the start of term.

'Mum,' he replied, 'I'll be the one doing the snapping.'

Sometimes it's hard to keep in mind that they're changing internally. One can make too much of the outward signs.

One day I come in and Peter intercepts me in the hall.

'Sssh!' he whispers. 'They're both reading *How to Train Your Dragon* books, while discussing the lesbian oral sex fantasy in *Black Swan*.'

Aaaaah.

Then, I'm working upstairs in my study when I hear an adult male voice in the hall. Peter is out for the day, and anyhow it sounds nothing like him.

I hold my breath, heart thumping, and listen.

This is the problem with working at home; people think the house is empty. And there's only one thing worse than coming home to find you've been burgled; it's being burgled while you're *in*.

I pick up my phone and put one finger on the 9.

Please don't let him come up here . . .

Then, as I'm about to start dialling, I hear:

'Mu-um!'

It can't be.

It is.

I go down to the kitchen to find Lawrence in his school blazer.

'Oh my God!' I say. 'It's you!'

'So it would appear.'

'But – your voice! It's so – *deep*. I didn't recognize you.'

He puts a piece of bread in the toaster. Has he not even *noticed*?

'I suppose I thought, you know, you'd go all squeaky first, like the burger guy in *The Simpsons*.'

'Seemingly not.'

I look at him afresh.

He has big shoulders and the beginnings of a moustache. In fact, he has changed completely. I mean, I knew about the shoulders, but that, with the Voice and the Height – and the Stubble – he has gone from being the second smallest boy in the class, a child convinced he would never grow, to – a not entirely hideous *young man*.

And he is still only thirteen.

When he gets in, Peter's not astonished at all.

'Well,' he says, 'I did grow five inches the year I turned fourteen.'

'Still, though.'

Dark facial hair does run in my family – as I can attest – but not height. We regard people who grow taller almost as supernatural phenomena, like those houseplants that get out of hand and take over a whole room. The people next door to Peter's aunty had a *Monsterosa Deliciosa* – or Swiss cheese plant – that grew right up one wall, across the ceiling, which was a good ten feet high at least, then down the other side. God knows what they fed it.

Peter was the same. He puts it down to spaghetti

and tuna, which had just come to Sheffield. And he took full advantage of his transformation.

'In the summer of 1969 I was fourteen, and the same height I am now (five foot eleven). My dad was working on the island of St Vincent, inspecting their education system. I went to visit him, and as an unaccompanied minor I had a dedicated air hostess who escorted me onto the plane at Heathrow. At JFK, where I had to change planes, she left me to amuse myself for an hour. So I put on my sunglasses, took out my cigarettes and went to the bar and had a beer.'

And this was New York, where the minimum drinking age was, and still is, twenty-one.

So when does a boy become a man?

My father was bar mitzvah'd at thirteen; from that point you're allowed to help lead religious services and are accountable for your actions. All in all, not a bad idea. But he never kept it up. My mother is a passionate atheist and we grew up secular, immune to the effect of our religious primary schools; we were unplagued by institutional bullshit but in the family, very short of rituals. So I quite fancy the idea of a coming-of-age celebration.

'Hey,' I say to Lawrence. 'Why don't we have a party? We could call it "Not the Calman-Grimsdale Bar Mitzvah". What d'you think? You could come for the first hour, then go off with your friends. It'd be fun! Yeah? What d'you think?'

'That is literally a Really, Really Terrible Idea.'

He butters his toast and takes his homework into the other room.

About a week later we have a row and I shout:

'Go to your room!'

And he looks down at me, and says:

'No.'

'So,' I say to Peter. 'What do we do now?'

'It'll be fine.'

'Well, I'm really glad we had this talk.'

Shortly after this, Lawrence and I have a day out together. A temporary lake has been put on the roof of the Hayward Gallery where you can have a short boat ride, and afterwards we go for lunch in the old film theatre cafe on the South Bank, where my father used to take me after we'd been to see Fred Astaire and Ginger Rogers musicals and early black and white animations.

I order a beer for me and a Coke for Lawrence, and when the waitress returns, she gives him the beer.

'Oh my God . . .!' I say.

'Wow,' he says.

She shrugs, swaps the drinks and ambles off.

We go out onto the Embankment and have a look at the bookstalls – briefly, because Lawrence is bored and if you force them it only puts them off – then go to another cafe for a hot chocolate.

'Check the price and I'll give you the money,' I say, because I think that if I don't give him the exact money he'll get ripped off, because when Lydia was eight she was cheated out of £5 by an ice-cream van person and I had to go back and demand it, even though I know that: (a) this happened not to him but his sister; and (b) he is no longer eight.

He comes back with the chocolate.

'How much was it?'

'Nothing.'

'What do you mean, nothing?'

'I mean it was free.'

'What? Why?'

'She said I was cute.'

I look over, and the pretty serving girl is still smiling in his direction.

'Bloody hell.'

I gaze at him, trying to process this.

'What?'

'Use that power wisely, boy, that's all.'

I don't think he has any idea yet what I mean.

*

As I'm not allowed a 'Not-the-Calman-Grimsdale-Bar-Mitzvah' party, and as the hot chocolate example – 'basically a story about how cute I am' – Lawrence vetoes as Too Embarrassing, I tell everyone I know about the beer. In the absence of a cultural rite of passage witnessed by the whole community it will have to do.

But life is lying in wait for us with an actual rite of passage that isn't very cute at all.

Lawrence and his friend J come back from the park with two girls we've never seen before. They fail my first test, by going straight past us into the garden without saying hello. As Miss Clavel puts it so succinctly in *Madeline,* in the middle of the night: something is not right.

The girls don't stay long, and after they and J have left, Lawrence comes and sits with us at the patio table and puts his head on his folded arms. Hmm, the boy lacks energy. In fact, he doesn't look at all well.

Peter and I go into a quick huddle in the kitchen, and as usual, handle the issue by arguing with each other.

'He's drunk, isn't he? Those girls have given them alcohol!'

So much for that talk I had with him two years ago about trust.

'Well let's not Make a Thing of It.'

'All right then – what *do* you want to do?'

'Let's just . . .'

'So you've no idea.'

While we're dithering, he sleeps it off: problem solved.

But no . . .

The next day, an anonymous young female rings the landline and asks for him. He's still at school, so I tell her that, and ask who's calling, and she says her name in a way that sounds as though she doesn't see why she should tell me.

I tell Lawrence.

'Where did you meet them, by the way?'

'At the park.'

'They're not from your school, though, are they?'

They turn out to be Year Nines from one of the girls' private schools – which I find shocking; you'd think that drunk or sober, they'd have at least been taught not to come into someone's house without saying hello.

The day after that, Lawrence tells us that the girls went round to J's house to invite him to go drinking with them again in the park, only it was 2.30 a.m. He not unreasonably said no, and they put a note through his door expressing their disappointment by calling him a Very Bad Word.

'Right, that's it!'

'What?'

'I'm going to talk to J's mother.'

'What? Why?'

'It's appalling the way they've behaved, especially to J, who's a lovely boy and just – doesn't deserve it.'

J's mother is a kind and sensible person who, in common with me, likes the odd drink or three, and is about as far from being a puritan as it is possible to get.

'I think we should ring their school,' I say, over a beer.

'Actually . . .' she says, 'I don't think we need to. I talked to J, and I think he's learned quite a big lesson over this.'

And since Peter agrees with her, I back down.

I'm left feeling envious that J and his mother had a Proper Talk about it and we didn't. And it still bridles, the way those brazen minxes marched past me without saying hello.

I'm so hung up on this I never think to ask where they got the booze, and it's only years later that Lawrence admits some of it came from here.

Ages 13 to 15: Route Master

Lydia is going to be thirteen. When she and Lawrence were small, displays of birthday one-upmanship were largely limited to a magician or, if you really pushed the boat out, a chap with a van of exotic animals chosen to startle the kids a bit without destroying the average middle-class living room. There was usually a tarantula. But since then, the stakes have shot up.

Recently a friend's daughter was invited to a sixteenth at which the guests each received a going-home present of the latest must-have: an iPod Shuffle. And I learn from a father in North London that his son's classmate is having the entire cast of *Thriller* – yes, the stage show based on the Michael Jackson album – to perform the whole thing at the stately home they've hired for his bar mitzvah. Not even that long ago the most opulent birthday treat Lawrence had been to was go-karting. Now everyone's Philip Green.

The challenge is to find a midway point between

Pass the Parcel and getting wasted. But we needn't worry.

'It's fine,' says Lydia: 'I already know what I'm doing.'

She invites her eight closest friends to Pizza Express with two provisos: we must pay but not go with them, and they must all – including the one boy in her crowd – be dressed as their interpretation of Lady Gaga.

'I'd give anything to be able to watch you all walk down there,' I say.

'Well you can't.'

As a concession she agrees to take some pictures on her present, a phone.

'But don't take it out in the street—'

'Because it'll get stolen: I *know*.'

I give her the cash for the meal.

'Don't forget to check the bill.'

'I *know*.'

'And leave 10 per cent – but round it up.'

'ALL RIGHT! JUST LEAVE ME ALONE!'

The thirteenth birthday, such a big deal when I was that age, is in reality less of a milestone than her first non-local bus journey, to a friend's house about half an hour away.

When they were small, they could make friends

213

with anyone inside a radius of about two miles; anything beyond that meant too much precious time in the car. But I'd always weaken and make exceptions for children we really liked. And Peter would take them anywhere – 'Sleepover in Glasgow? Righto!' – to maintain his position as Top Parent.

Lawrence has a new friend who lives a train-and-bus ride away. Or it's an hour's drive across the river, and the parking is hideous. I'm so anxious about parking tickets I have to hope the clearly interesting other mother doesn't offer me a coffee. Then, just as we're hoping they solve the problem for us by moving away, he suddenly masters the route.

'And remember, always sit *downstairs*, because—'

'The psychos are always upstairs: I KNOW!'

This has been my policy since a stabbing on the number 37 after one passenger asked another not to throw chips. In my day, you could walk clear across the West End facing no greater danger than someone falling onto you accidentally from a pub doorway. When I was fourteen, I was once walking back from a party, about four miles away, when two policemen pulled up and offered me a lift; they were on their way back to the police station at the end of our road. When we arrived the driver asked for a kiss, which back then didn't seem unreasonable.

To help me not worry too much, Lawrence sends me a text from his new phone:

Staying late to have unprotected sex and accept sweets from strangers.

Oddly enough, this works far better than Peter saying: 'Stop worrying.'

At the Temple of Cake

Lawrence and I go down to our local high street together, not to get a haircut, or school shoes, or games kit for sports he's never going to play. We're going out for coffee.

We sit in the window of the place with a French name, owned by a Cypriot and staffed by Czechs, watching the pavement traffic. There's a noticeable contrast between the youngish nicely dressed women with pushchairs and the slightly battered-looking old men: the neighbourhood past and present.

'There's still a launderette here,' I observe, 'but for how long?'

'You mean by the time we leave, will it have become an overpriced maternity wear shop?'

We get our coffees and as we sit there, something lovely happens.

I feel the spirit – or no, it's more like the *atmosphere* – of my father, who died seventeen years ago, sitting with us.

He used to take me out for tea and cakes, a ritual whose restorative qualities he first experienced during the drudgery of National Service. Imagine how it must have felt to escape marching and being shouted at for the maternal attentions of warm, buttery waitresses with tea in a pot and a home-made teacake or scone. I was three when he first took me to Patisserie Valerie, where Madame Valerie herself received me, a goddess of plenty at her temple of cake, in an ambience of vanilla, lemon and chocolate tinged with just a hint of cigarette smoke. If I ever imagined heaven, it looked and smelled like that.

And I'm filled with a sense of peace and well-being.

And for a little while I feel that I am my father, and Lawrence is me. If I can manage not to mention homework or tidying, it will be perfect.

Dad, I wish I could tell you I did have children after all – despite your telling me to – and I'm glad I did.

'Mum?' says Lawrence. 'Are you OK? *Hello?*'

'Mm, just – enjoying being here with you.'

Ages 14 & 15: Relationships Through the Ages

We ask Lawrence what he wants for his fifteenth birthday.

'A bass. I know the one I want: all you have to do is pay for it.'

'That sounds wonderfully effortless. Why a bass?'

'Well, it sounds cool. And it has only four strings, so I figure it might be a bit easier than a regular guitar.'

Ah, that's my boy.

We ask the school to find him a teacher. They take six weeks to get back to us, and when they do it's a guitar teacher – not the same thing at all. Meanwhile, he starts teaching himself using online tabs and YouTube.

'As most people choose the guitar,' I say, 'bassists are always in demand.'

'Let's not get carried away.'

'Sorry.'

The bass has a particular resonance for me.

We sit down together at the computer and watch clips of top practitioners around the world.

'My first true love was a bass player,' I say, without thinking.

'Really?'

And before I can qualify this – or even think how I feel about it – he has typed in his name and there he is, performing on *Top of the Pops* in 1981.

The intervening decades fall away. It's so like seeing someone come back from the dead that I feel quite shaken. I ended it because of a misunder-standing I've felt badly about for over thirty years. I thought he preferred someone else, felt too devastated to talk to him, and just shut him out. On the other hand, I learned just about enough from the debacle to stay in therapy long enough to start confronting my fears, get married, have children and actually stay married.

So far.

'Mum?'

'Mm? What?'

'He looks really cool.'

What a relief: in 1981, most of us looked rubbish.

'So what did he play?'

'What d'you mean?'

'What bass?'

'I've no idea.'

He looks aghast.

'For someone who went out with a bass player, you really don't know much about it.'

Shortly after this, he gets a girlfriend himself.

She is polite and very pretty, with porcelain skin. Despite her petite figure she likes food and eats healthily, so instantly gets my vote. She doesn't talk as much we do, but then no one does. Hang on – an awful thought occurs: she might be nervous around me. Me!

So I make an effort to reduce my domestic foot-print, and not to be so *blunt* or *frank* or LOUD all the time, and strive to distil my overbearing presence into something benign but not bland, which means I end up saying:

'Would you like a drink? How about something to eat?' about fifteen times a day, like a Jewish RoboMum, while my non-Jewish half snaps: 'Shut up! She prob-ably just wants you to leave her alone.'

And in a moment of unwelcome clarity I realize that, to her, my whole identity is Boyfriend's Mother. There is nothing – not lines on the neck, not grey roots or a stomach like badly packed shopping – as ageing as that. It feels doom-laden, like the moment in every female actor's career when they see the dread words on the audition script, brutally highlighted: *The Mother*. Once you pass into that glamour-free zone, there's no coming back; it's supporting roles only from now on.

'I'm not sure I'm ready for this,' I tell a friend.

'Don't worry,' she says. 'They're fifteen: it's not as though they're going to get *married*.'

No, though for the next three years it is a little bit like it.

The only unsettling moments come when I mention that Lawrence has a girlfriend and at least three people we know say, with undisguised eagerness:

'Ooh! Are they having sex?'

But here's the plus side – a very big plus in my view: it's clear that our son is naturally monogamous. This is brilliant! And I can think of another massive advantage this will bring.

During one of our regular coffees together, I say to our friend Patrick, who also has a boy and a girl:

'Hey, I know how to solve the problem of boys and porn: get them in a relationship! No substitute for the Real Thing, eh?'

'OMG, you actually think it's one or the other?!'

And he laughs, leaning forward till he's almost out of his seat.

Orange is Not the Only Black

I'm making an effort to spend more time with Lydia, now fourteen, which largely involves watching more television. It's on the advice of my friend Teresa, whose children seem to adore her. So I've decided to do what she does.

'What's the number one tip?'

'Be interested in what *they're* interested in.'

'Right!'

But why does that have to be television? I hear you say.

Because the alternative is *Minecraft*.

And I love watching TV; it entertains and informs you, and asks for nothing back. The interactive generation don't know what they're missing.

Luckily our kids are old enough to remember the old, traditional amusements, and have no trouble sitting passively on a sofa, although Lydia will insist on making something at the same time. There are always three of you in any relationship: you, her and the sewing machine. She can't watch the subtitles on Scandi noir because she's looking down most of the time, and the more suspenseful scenes are frequently drowned out by the sound of *ka-chunking*.

'I don't mind what we watch,' she says, 'so long as it's not about serial killers, corruption or floods.'

I don't know what she has against floods.

She's already on series two of *Buffy the Vampire Slayer*, so I plunge in with that. Despite its ancient vintage – it began in 1997 – it's held up very well. It doesn't matter that I've already missed a few episodes, as the plots are quite similar; there's something untoward about the new student at the high school, English Giles looks something up in his Old Library, new student turns out to be a vampire out to kill Buffy, a battle ensues and she wins – though only just!

Then after about eight or nine episodes of that, she shows me a new drama, *Orange is the New Black*. But my internal auto-correct refuses to separate it lexically from Jeanette Winterson's classic *Oranges are Not the Only Fruit*, so I can't help calling it *Orange is Not the Only Black*. And once it's gone into my brain like that I really can't seem to change it, which really irritates both her *and* Lawrence, who likes it too. *And* it's something my mother does.

But in fact it doesn't matter what I call it, because

in the second or third episode, the unpopular new inmate is served a used tampon at lunch. This being an American prison it's in a bun, but still.

'I don't want you to think I'm – disapproving,' I say. 'I just, I'm just not sure I can—'

'It's OK, Mum.'

'And I'm definitely *not* criticizing the lesbian sex in the showers . . .'

Which is pretty explicit.

'It's *OK*!'

Now I've annoyed her again.

The next time I ask what she's watching, it's another new show: *Game of Thrones*.

'I'll give it a try.'

After all, it can't possibly be more explicit or outlandish than *Orange is Not the Only Black*.

In episode one, a girl with silver hair is betrayed into marriage by her brother, teaches her barbaric new husband how to have face-forward sex, then, cheered on by his men, eats the raw heart of a horse.

'If you don't like this,' says Lydia, 'we can always watch something else.'

Actually it's the wanton use of the subjunctive that gets me. Daenerys Targaryen, the silver-haired one, says – while being taken from behind:

'I would look upon your face.'

And thus invents the missionary position.

'Well,' I say, 'maybe something else? Just, you know, this time.'

She flicks through the programmes she's recorded on the hard disk.

'*Supervet* – that's good.'

We watch Noel the silky-voiced Irish vet surgically attach high-tech orthopaedic implants to the stumps of the amputated legs of dogs. No bloody, sinewy detail is left out.

'Er . . . I'm sorry, but I feel a bit sick.'

'OK – this is an animal programme with no operations in.'

It's called *Animal Madhouse*. A dog is brought to the vet repeatedly nibbling its own willy.

'Urgh', I say, 'that's disgusting!'

'They don't have opposable thumbs, so I guess this is their only option.'

'I'm sorry, I just can't . . .'

'OK . . . *Embarrassing Bodies* . . .?'

'All right, let's try that.'

We watch a man with a bent penis and a woman with excess flab on her vulva – quite a surprising amount of it – bravely submit themselves to examination. The surgery is at least off camera, but I cannot quite take the cushion away from my face.

'OK . . .' says Lydia. 'What about this?'

'*Tattoo Fixers*? What's it like?'

'It's really good: you'll like it, I promise.'

I watch as a series of well-meaning victims with tattoos that *don't* look like Bob Marley, Elvis, Nelson Mandela and, again, a penis, troop in to have them inked over with more acceptable images, like roses. There's also a cute-looking receptionist who does nothing but come in as they reveal their various epidermal catastrophes, and say:

'Oh, my God . . .'

'Oh, my God . . .' I say too.

The tattooists are a sympathetic bunch with cool hairstyles and some very competent tattoos of their own, but again, I cannot look.

Eventually I say:

'How about something I've recorded? I've got one or two saved for you, actually.'

We flick along: I stop at *Jane Eyre* with Michael Fassbender and Mia Wasikowska.

'This is good.'

'I'm not really in the mood for a film.'

'OK, how about the Oliver Postgate documentary?'

The one about the making of *Ivor the Engine*, *The Clangers* and other timeless classics of British animation. Without them there would be no *Wallace and Gromit*, or *Shaun the Sheep*. Without—

'I've seen it.'

I know, but I can't delete it. Just having it there makes the world seem a better, less threatening place.

'We met Peter Firmin, d'you remember? You showed him the Baby Clanger you made.'

'I *know*! I was *there*. What are you telling me for? And it was *Tiny* Clanger.'

'I'm not, I'm just – remembering.'

A tense silence descends.

And it dawns on me that the distance from those adorable creatures on their small planet to bent penises, lesbian shower sex and the eating of raw horses' hearts has been a good deal shorter than I anticipated. In three years Lydia has moved on considerably, and I'm still trying – and she might say, failing – to catch up.

In a year from now, she will go to Comic Con as Rhaegal the Dragon from *Game of Thrones*, with her friend Freya as Daenerys, Mother of Dragons and Queen of the Random Use of the Subjunctive. She gets into her shimmering green and bronze costume with handsewn, foldable wings. And Tiny Clanger and I stand in the hall and wave goodbye, as she extends her wings and heads for the train.

Festival Dad

As Lydia's lot reach Year Ten, they're encouraged to do the Duke of Edinburgh Award, known popularly as D of E. There are three levels – Bronze, Silver and Gold – designed to promote teamwork, self-reliance and walking in very wet socks. Lawrence has done it up to Bronze, then dropped it. Lydia can't wait to do the whole thing.

Those who complete all three levels – hiking twenty kilometres a day for four days with a pack that's a quarter of their weight, camping in the wild, learning a skill and volunteering – get to go to Buckingham Palace to receive their awards. If she gets a move on she may even qualify before the actual D of E becomes too ancient to hand them out.

'I've already got my skill,' she says.

'What's that?'

'Sewing, of course.'

She's been sewing since she discovered her thumbs. So not strictly speaking a *new* skill.

'Hmm, OK. What about the volunteering?'

Having not seen her volunteer too often for anything round the house, I'm somewhat sceptical.

'Freya works at a charity shop. I can do it with her – and get first pick of the clothes. Win-win!'

I prepare to sneer, but when I hear how far they have to walk before pitching their tents, quite possibly in the dark, my cynicism evaporates. I haven't seen her so motivated since the campaign to get a rabbit.

'I wish we'd had D of E,' I tell Peter. 'It would have been so good for me – and all of us floppy creative types. It would have made me more, you know, self-reliant.'

'Yeah, less useless.'

At my school pretty much everyone was either academic, academic-and-musical, academic-and-sporty or academic-and-arty. I was in a very small subset of girls who weren't any of those, who bunked off games and weren't even going to university, whom the school put up with in a bemused sort of way, as you indulge a pointless but diverting pet.

ephanie Calman*

'You're right,' he says. 'D of E would probably have made you less feeble.'

But there's a hitch.

It's oversubscribed. The group is full to bursting, and anyone who doesn't get in must do the compulsory alternative.

'And what's that?'

'Combined Cadet Force.'

Er, I don't think so.

We've seen them, marching in uniform to the local war memorial on Remembrance Day – the Army in brown, Navy in navy and Air Force in dashing light blue. And while it's very moving and all that, I really cannot have any child of mine participating in military manoeuvres, even if the only piece of equipment they're holding is a flag.

'We're happy for you to get up at dawn to walk twelve miles with a huge backpack and put up tents on the sides of mountains,' I say, 'but no playing soldiers.'

'But I TOLD you: D of E is FULL so I have to DO THIS!'

'I'm sorry but that's the end of it.'

Even Peter, who hates refusing her anything, tacitly agrees.

And to conclusively put the lid on it I email the school:

Dear Squadron Leader Miss XX copied to Head of Year Mrs Y,

Lydia is very keen on outdoor activities and camping, but the military nature of CCF does not appeal to her, nor does it fit with our values. As you know, she has a very full extra-curricular life with gymnastics, climbing courses, music, designing and making clothes, but as the available time shrinks even further in the period building up to GCSEs, we are not happy for her to have to take on another activity that she is not motivated to do, and which we cannot support. Is it possible for her to be reconsidered for D of E?

To which the answer is: No.

'Thank God that's sorted,' I tell Peter, and make a note to award myself another Effectiveness badge.

Later that very day, Lydia comes in from school and as the front door swings shut, a happy voice trills up the stairs:

'Mum! Dad! I'VE JOINED THE NAVY!!'

The only other choice, if we really *really* object, is volunteering.

'What, like working in the charity shop?'

'No! *Helping* people.'

Royal Navy Combined Cadet Force subsidized by the Ministry of Defence it is, then.

*

231

Now, in a surprise development, Lawrence has also begun to express an interest in the outdoors.

It's six years since he was brought home from Hippy Camp, and his aversion to sleeping in the rain has faded.

How strange. Why?

He wants to go to his first music festival.

But unlike all his friends who are going he was born in August and is not yet sixteen.

'Maybe I should go,' says Peter.

'What?'

'Well, I've inspected the website and I can't see how he's going to get in otherwise.'

'You, a fifty-six-year-old man, want to go to a music festival.'

He looks quite good for his age, but 'Festival Dad'? With grey ponytail, batik shirt and floppy, drawstring trousers . . . And a tie-dyed poncho for evening wear.

'Maybe he should just wait until he's old enough to get in normally,' I say.

'But all his friends are going. After their GCSEs – and all that.'

'I thought the post-GCSE treat was going to be coming to France with us.'

As soon as I say this, I feel like some pathetic

creature whose child is their whole life. I can feel my firstborn starting to slip away, and it's not happening the way I thought it would.

'Yes, but this is the Treat with his Friends.'

Of course. And he can't go because he's under age. Or he can, but only with a parent.

'I knew it,' I say. 'This is what comes of having an August baby.'

'Don't start: it's not about *you*.'

'Well, it's not my fault he's the youngest in the year.'

Actually it sort of is. If I'd moved the C-section to the following week he'd have been the eldest in his year.

'Look,' says Peter. 'It's all going to be fine. He can get in with me to the family section, then peel off with his mates.'

'Then what'll you do? Just come back? You're going to drive all the way to Suffolk, and straight back again?'

A pause.

'We thought I might stay a couple of days.'

We?

Lydia comes in.

'Hey Dad: Georgie's *definitely* up for coming with us!'

I shoot Peter a look. He looks at her. I look at her. She looks at *me* – accusingly.

'What?'

She and Georgie are both nearly fifteen. So also under age.

'So let me get this right,' I say. '*You're* going so that Lawrence can go. And *Lydia's* going so that *you* can go.'

'Yes,' says Peter.

'No,' says Lydia, at the same time.

'And Georgie's going so that Lydia has some company under the age of sixty.'

It goes without saying she won't be invited to 'hang' with Lawrence and his friends.

'I'm not sixty for another four years yet.'

'Whatever! No one cares.'

'The point is no one will look as though they're going with their dad.'

'Exactly!'

'Even though they are.'

'I'm not getting involved in this argument,' says Lydia, slipping out of the room. She's picked up her father's ability to detach herself from disputes that she totally *is* involved in, and just float away.

This is tricky. On the one hand, I'm faintly appalled

by the thought of my ageing spouse grooving in a field. Would *you* want to emerge from your tent to see your own parent dancing to Clean Bandit with luminous hair and waving glow sticks, trying to 'blend in', let alone – don't even *think* it – sharing a spliff with someone called Cleopatra who reads crystals in Shepton Mallet?

'Your view of festivals, by the way,' says Lawrence, 'is about a million years out of date.'

On the other hand, I'm far *more* panicked by the prospect of my daughter and her friend in a tent, basically a large *bag*, exposed to thousands of semi-clothed, off-their-face males.

'There's a separate family section,' says Peter. 'With parents and kids and so on.'

'Yes, thank you: I know what a family is.'

It means both our kids can have this great experience and I don't have to go anywhere near it.

I'm starting to come round to the idea.

'Don't worry,' says Peter. 'The family campsite's cordoned off from the rest of it, with showers and proper loos – with soft toilet paper. And lots of craft activities, like making string from nettle stems.'

'You're kidding.'

'Lydia's *really* looking forward to it.'

He's right: sleeping in the rough and making stuff out of twigs, plus music: it's her perfect dream of Hippy Camp grown up.

'It's not just music,' adds Peter. 'There's comedy and poetry and stuff. It'll be great. You should come!'

It's been over twenty years; does he even know me?

I have camped once in my life, as a child in Scotland – where the gorgeous scenery is guarded in summer by hordes of midges, so the choice is being frozen or bitten, plus rained on. We spent most of it in the car, eating chips. And my most feral experience was when my friends pulled me through a hedge into an open-air concert when we had no tickets. I had on a mohair jumper and spent the whole time looking over my shoulder in case the police had analysed the fluff stuck to the hawthorn and were coming over the grass to arrest me.

There is nothing that appeals to me about sleeping on the ground in a room made of cloth. It's like trying to reverse evolution:

'Hey, let's go Neolithic! We can eat raw meat and die in childbirth!'

Also, my family have already roughed it. My grandmother didn't get shot at running from the Tsar's border guards so I could queue for water and sleep in my clothes.

Peter says:

'Georgie's parents think it's a *great* idea.'

I bet they do. Who isn't in favour of someone taking their offspring somewhere they themselves would never set foot?

'I will find something else to do,' I say stiffly.

And if anything *does* go wrong – dubious substances ingested, unsafe sexual encounters in the mud, it will be on his watch.

They set off in a stuffed car with Georgie, Lawrence's mate Will, a tiny pop-up tent for them, a large two-room tent for Peter and the girls, a small Campingaz stove, two pans, three mugs, a cafetiere, a pack of Lavazza, about twenty sachets of instant porridge and a strangely heavy backpack which has also appeared.

Peter sends his first text.

Am NOT the oldest one here! Some have long grey hair and beards.

Lyd loving music and craft – plus Eddie Izzard, beat boxing + doughnuts.

And L?

Glimpsed him once, bare chested in neon warpaint.

He's been instructed to bring the strangely heavy backpack round to the other section to hand through the fence at nightfall. It's full of beer. Word spreads, for Lawrence tells him:

'A guy has literally just come up to me and said: "I hear you can get stuff in" . . .'

So, Festival Dad meets *The Shawshank Redemption* is a huge success.

'In the dark I was less conscious of my age,' he reports afterwards.

'What, like that cartoon: "On the internet no one knows you're a dog"?'

'Not like that at all. And the girls were fine about being with me.'

He made sure not to so much as nod his head to any music.

At the end of the three days they went round to get the boys, Peter keeping his distance so as not to embarrass them with his presence in front of their mates.

'Actually he looked rather relieved to see me, given the challenge of packing up camp in his fragile condition.'

'You didn't do it all for them, did you?'

'No, no, of course not.'

He and Will were fast asleep in the back of the car before they were even out of the site, and remained so all the way home. When they stopped for petrol he sent me a picture of them, slumped in their seats, their heads on one side, like two giant toddlers who'd been finger-painting.

I hate to admit it, but he's pulled it off.

I wonder how he'll feel next year, when they can go without him?

Ages 15 & 16:
Uber Your Own Piglet

Once upon a time, the children used to say adorable, slightly inaccurate things that I wrote down in a notebook, like 'uppa-plane' for aeroplane, because it goes *up*. Aaaah.

Now, Peter and I say similar things, but the line between amusing parental malapropisms and the failure to know stuff is unsettlingly thin.

For example, there's an American woman on the radio talking about Play-Doh, which seems an odd subject for Radio 4. Has someone left it on a *commercial* station? Lydia . . .! Then the woman says he was an Ancient Greek philosopher. What? Oh, wait . . .

I tell the kids, and they find it quite amusing. I've not got it wrong because of my age; they might just as easily have misheard it like that too.

Lawrence is becoming quite interested in food, so I take him out for a treat to a glamorous new restaurant full of twinkling lights, pale wood and large chunks of eucalyptus. For his 'small plate' – because *starter* is so last week – the waitress grates some wasabi root against a slab of something that looks like the asbestos tiles we used to use in the school physics lab, and gestures at a tiny square dish.

'And that's the soy sauce.'

It seems to be just a thin layer in the bottom and it's turquoise: a fashionable kind of soy sauce in a 'statement' colour? I say nothing. Lawrence doesn't react either. Then she pours in some brown liquid out of a small pottery bottle and melts away.

'Ah!' says Lawrence. '*That's* the soy sauce.'

'I thought it might be that blue stuff,' i.e. the glaze, I say, relieved.

'Me too!'

For a minute there I was nervous.

'Ha ha,' says Lydia later. 'Well, I used to think "Silicon Valley" was where everyone had had plastic surgery.'

Which is completely understandable; why wouldn't it be a place where all the inhabitants have smooth faces and abnormally round tits?

And then I tell her that while looking for my gloves I've found a business card in Lawrence's spare jacket belonging to 'The Dealer' – I didn't know they had them. And she looks up the url on it and tells me it's dealer as in *deals*, i.e. special offers on meals that, in this case, also support local charities.

And don't I feel stupid!

But using the wrong word for something everyday and *obvious* is not the same thing.

Thinking of an image we passed in the street somewhere, I say:

'I liked that music notice we saw the other day.'

And Lawrence says:

'Do you mean *poster*?'

And I think: of course I do; I know what a bloody poster is. Also, which is worrying, I didn't even intend to say it, it just came out. But sometimes I get so nervous about sounding out of touch it makes me say the wrong thing, as if I'm in the Resistance and am going to personally lose us the war.

'*Le petit oiseau est dans l'arbre*,' says my contact.

'Er . . . *oui*?'

Then when caught by the Gestapo I'd be shot for not handing over the codes, because I really *wouldn't* be able to remember them. On the plus side, I'd be remembered as 'terbly terbly brave', though dead.

'Music notice' indeed! Next I'll be asking them how to download 'Whats*Upp*'. Possibly I already have.

Lately our conversations have been derailed quite

often by detours like this. You'd think their irritation would have died out by now; since they're on the verge of adulthood, not twelve. I can see how at *that* age kids want to show how up to the minute and sophisticated they are, and how out of touch and lame their parents. But we've surely long passed that point; we totally know that they're young yet mature and worldly-wise and we're middle-aged and bumbling, and so don't need to be pulled up on every tiny mistake.

But I'm wrong.

And I recognize Lawrence's contrasting reactions to Play-Doh and 'music notice' from when I used to snap at my mother: it's fear.

I couldn't bear her making mistakes because they were proof that she was getting older and would at some point start to forget things permanently, and eventually deteriorate, perhaps even into dementia as her mother did.

Peter has a different theory.

'They've got to get annoyed with us, haven't they?'

Er, have they? Why?

'If we never got annoyed with our parents, and went on liking them unreservedly, we'd never lead independent lives.'

David Attenborough says it's hardwired into us,

the mechanism that enables us to leave the pride and set up our own. So I suppose it must be true.

'Yeah,' I say, 'but that's more of a male-challenging-dominant-male thing, though, like stags and gorillas and whatever, not snapping at the chief lion for saying "music notice".'

'Chief lion?'

'Pride leader or whatever. So, me.'

But he does have a point.

And I wonder if this process has become trickier.

In ye olde dayes it was straightforward. You put on your high-heel sneakers and the latest 45, and at least one parent would be guaranteed to jump up, whip the needle off and slam the door, muttering that Elvis was a degenerate and Little Richard not only a *negro* but a blatant wearer of *women's make-up*, and that music had been rubbish ever since Handel. Job done. And if by any chance that didn't do the trick, a Ban the Bomb poster in the front room window would usually sort it.

And then in my day there was punk, which made it even easier. A random safety-pin or two in the school uniform was enough to get even a liberal teacher breathing a bit faster, so you could have all your rebelling done by break, and not even have to smoke in the playground – which was handy if you didn't really like punk, which most of us didn't, and didn't actually smoke either, only took it up now and then to stick it to The Man. Or, in the case of my school, the Actually Quite Reasonable Woman. My friend Tilly had her own range of civil disobedience techniques, of which the most satisfying was to smile at the fuming teacher and say:

'And I love you too . . .'

Rebellion-wise, my parents presented something of a challenge. My mother read books like *Deschooling Society* and listened to Shostakovich and Nina Simone. And even my father, who was quite strict, had a goatee and interviewed jazz musicians for the papers. So, there was no mileage there. Even if I'd come home with a Val Doonican album they would have been baffled but not annoyed. And anyhow, I really did like the same music as them. I came into school one day looking gloomy, and one of the other girls asked what the matter was.

'Oh, nothing. Just – Duke Ellington died.'

'*Who?*'

But now, the poor old teenagers really have got their work cut out.

'Portia and I are so close! We tell each other everything – and she's always borrowing my stuff' – for which read: 'Teenagers find me just fascinating, and did I mention I'm a size 8?'

Yeah, you did.

Listen, lady: just because she sometimes nicks your jumpers and leaves them at parties – where they get vodka and several types of ash trodden into them – doesn't mean you're her bestie. Person up, and make your own friends.

When the kids were younger, Peter and I once went to a smart country hotel for a night, with a private hot-tub outside our room; not really my thing, sitting in a large bowl of water without my flannel, but quite romantic with a glass of champagne. And as we gazed up at the stars, he said:

'You know what I'm thinking? The kids would have loved this.'

Sometimes I just don't know how the teenagers of today will manage.

Still, Lawrence is rising to the challenge:

'Why do you just assume I'm not going to lock the door?'

'I don't, I'm just –'

'Why do you just assume I'm going to take drugs?'

Actually I never have assumed that: he just throws it in for good measure.

And:

'Why do you assume I'm more likely to be killed

on the way home from a party at 1 a.m. than at midnight?'

I don't believe this either; I just like to know when to start worrying.

His other technique is to remind me that much of what I know or have to say is irrelevant since the world – at some indeterminate recent point roughly coincidental with the coming of the internet – has become a Completely Different Place.

Take relationships.

A lovely young woman we know in her twenties has been telling me that she really wants to meet someone, but that the idea of going on Tinder makes her 'blood run cold'. And I see her point: this unnatural selection is anathema to those of us who came of age choosing a mate the civilized way, by taking a single drunken look at them across a smoke-filled room.

'This emphasis on choosing people based purely on looks,' I say. 'From a tiny image on a phone that you glance at for five seconds. It doesn't get you anywhere. I mean, people are still people.'

And Lawrence says:

'What does that even *mean*?'

'That they don't change. Relationships are much the same as they always were.'

He gives me his ultra-weary look, like someone at the post office being asked for the tenth time that day if they have passport forms, next to a huge sign saying: 'We do not have passport forms'.

'They're *so not*.'

'They really *are*.'

And so on.

At his age I had to listen to older people all the time, telling me what was what. Now it's *our* turn to say what's what, they get all their information from bloody Reddit.

I trudge wearily into the other room and put on the TV, feeling like a junior minister on *Newsnight* who finds that not only do they not know anything about their own portfolio, whatever they say makes things worse because their actual purpose is in fact not to run a department, but to be publicly humiliated simultaneously on all media. Luckily, for a bit of light relief there's a ten-part documentary series just beginning on the Vietnam War.

Peter says this is definitely part of The Process. Even in his family, where everyone was very sane and polite, he still had to break out and do things his own way.

'My father was relatively normal but I still found him irritating,' he says.

He died just before we met, but sounds like a jolly good sort.

'Yes, but sometimes he was just so – you know, *cautious*. Like when I was buying my first flat, and he said, "Whatever you do, make sure it's a new one, because old buildings need so much maintenance." And I just wanted to say: "Oh, for God's sake!"'

'Well, my parents weren't normal at all,' I say, 'and I quite often wanted to kill them.'

In my family the adults left home first. My father moved out when I was five. My mother waited, somewhat grudgingly, till my sister and I had finished school. In the months before she left, she would snarl at me that she couldn't wait to get away, out of horrible London and off to the country. To be fair, I think it was London she hated more than me, though I was horrible – and I would scream:

'WELL FUCKING GO THEN!'

I hadn't even considered trivial details like how we would pay the rent; all I wanted was for her to leave so my sister and I could have the place to ourselves. Even when she gave me the sitting room so I no longer had to share a bedroom, I don't think my behaviour improved.

The usual thing to do in that situation was – and is – to run off to your dad's. It's the compensation you get for having divorced parents: a choice of house to argue in. But my father had a terrible temper, triggered by hunger, insomnia, deadlines, lateness – I had to be in by ten thirty – and my stepmother. They both always wanted their own way but had no nego-tiation skills. They were like a fringe production of *Who's Afraid of Virginia Woolf* with a bonus: they could do it without being drunk. Plus, he never liked my boyfriends.

'The court says you have to stay with your father every Friday night to Sunday night till you're sixteen,' reiterated my mother, who didn't want me staying in the flat alone, but also didn't want to give up her child-free weekends – a much under-publicized upside of divorce. She lived part-time in Kent with her boyfriend, a man who didn't blow up all the time like Dad, but saved up his anger for long, tight-lipped silences followed by the occasional rampage when he would pull up her flowers.

'So you have to go.'

'FUCKING MAKE ME!'

Peter finds all this quite uplifting.

'Compared with your lot,' he says, 'we're really not doing badly at all.'

After a final row at my father's I walked out, and life became much calmer. Living at home the whole week I could at last enjoy civilized evenings at the pub without having to leave at ten, and sometimes a lock-in or an all-nighter with mates. One of them had an open house policy endorsed by his parents, ageing hippies who smoked quite a lot of dope themselves and never bothered us. And apart from a couple of druggies who were always too out of it to hold a conversation or otherwise participate properly, we were pretty moderate in our appetites. I did once share a bed with two of the lads, an actor and a musician. But after a promising start self-consciousness set in, and we couldn't work out how to have sex with three of us, so we gave up and went to sleep.

Still, I'd always thought I was the Worst Teenager Ever, until I heard about Peter's friends. For such a polite, house-trained individual, he had a pretty wild peer group. Nowadays, kids seem to be either properly criminal or ridiculously well behaved. But until about thirty years ago there was a rich seam of misbehaviour in between.

He had two friends who prised the badges off the cars of all their prep school teachers, then were caught trying to hide the evidence by burying them. Another friend set fire to his classroom when he was ten. At his mildly progressive boarding school a sixteen-year-old girl who got As for everything pushed the head of Chemistry into the swimming pool – in front of his own wife and kids. All of them went on to have careers and become parents themselves.

There was also the *father* of one of his friends, who, as a youth in the 1930s, climbed into a parked country bus and let off the brake, whereupon it rolled down a hill and into the river. He was expelled and given a police caution, before later becoming a museum curator and highly respected expert on the Renaissance.

Peter's school had outdoor provision for some pupils to keep pets, but strictly of the small fluffy variety. One day a new boy arrived for the sixth form with a piglet, which he hid among the hamsters and rabbits, where it became a celebrity yet somehow remained incognito until half-term, when he was asked to remove it. But his parents lived abroad and anyway he had no transport. Eventually he persuaded one of the day girls to take it; her parents had a place with a paddock. He made the arrangements, and all went well until one Saturday afternoon, when those working quietly in the library were disturbed by the most dreadful, blood-curdling squeals.

It was the piglet, being enticed into the boot of a minicab.

Sadly its fate is not known. Nowadays, the parents

would probably drop everything to come and get it. In fact, I can definitely imagine Lydia ringing from some far-flung animal refuge to ask if we can drive a hundred miles to pick up her and a traumatized goat. Perhaps we modern parents would do well to consider an updated equivalent of 'paddle your own canoe': Uber your own piglet.

But we're *not* Pushover Parents. Over the years we've said *No* to – among other things: party bags, bouncy castles, crop tops, a puppy, a kitten, a rabbit, scooters, a trampoline, a radio-controlled Dalek, cycling on public roads, premature phones, navel piercings and a llama.

Still – to us – Lawrence and Lydia and their friends seem incredibly good. Most of them barely ever step out of line. Yet surely it's in the human spirit to rebel; there must be an evolutionary advantage to not doing as you're told. Look at the escapers from Colditz, or the World Trade Center and Grenfell Tower: you want to be one of those who ignore the commands and get out; more crucially, in future you want your kids to be. They *need* to be.

My father used to tell me that Jews survive 'because of our stubbornness', and I agree. In me, though, it's a bit diluted, because he married my mother, who isn't Jewish, and is morally brave but when faced with a superior physical force – such as bullying neighbours or a tall hedge – tends to back down. So I'm stroppy only when not scared, which isn't much use. I'd love kids in general to have the courage and *initiative*, but without the bolshiness and *yelling*. Sometimes they're so angry with you they stop making sense. The daughter of a friend of Peter's, in the middle of a huge screaming match when she was about fourteen, suddenly accused him of being a 'wrinkled old penis'. Not having, *being*.

But must we really go through this? You don't hear gazelles, bats or hippopotamuses screaming at each other before they go off and build their own burrows or whatever. Even octopuses, who it's now known squirt water at people they don't like, at least refrain from slamming doors and shouting, 'Thanks for ruining my life!'

And the blackbirds, blue tits and so on who live in our garden, one minute they're building their nests, then you hear a bit of cheeping – then that's it: gone without a single twig thrown. You never even see them fledge, let alone have to listen to:

'Tidy this bloody nest! There's feathers and bits of half-eaten worm everywhere.'

Followed by:

'I'm fledging anyway. You're such a vulture, swooping down on me all the time.'

'Shut your beak, you bloody cuckoo.'

'I can't believe you just called me that.'

And so on.

And when they *do* reach the next stage, I really want to get it right. I'm aiming to be somewhere between those people who disappear for the weekend leaving their sixteen-year-olds to live on popcorn and ketamine, and the woman I heard about recently who has her son's food delivered to him at his halls of residence by Ocado. I mean, why not cut out the middle man and just take it yourself? Bring the condoms while you're at it. Oh no, wait: he won't be able to have sex BECAUSE YOU'RE THERE.

Then, when they move out, having supported but never suffocated them, I'll be the adored, indispensable mother, who gets thanked tearfully in their Oscar or Nobel speeches, whom they still turn to for Advice on Life.

Except I won't be, because they hate that. As Lawrence said to me recently:

'Can we just chat for once, without you giving me Talks on Life?'

And Lydia just runs away the minute she senses the threat of a DMC.

'What's that?'

'Deep and Meaningful Conversation.'

What the hell am I meant to do with all this *stuff* I've learned?

At least when they do go, I'm *fairly* certain I won't be doing what my grandmother did, namely fall against the door clutching her chest and cry at my aunt, who was finally leaving to get married:

'You've killed me!'

My aunt was thirty-seven.

Peter says:

'We just need to be like my sister.'

She's always done everything right, been supportive but detached, loving but not clingy. She's never criticized her sons' choices, always welcomed them back when they came home for a while, and not once tried to make them feel bad for moving away.

Now her first grandchild has just been born in Sydney, eleven thousand miles away.

So that's what you get for doing everything right.

But is all this stress and conflict really new? I know childhood was only invented once they were let out of the mills and mines, but adolescence has always been with us.

'Mum, I don't want to be a pagan any more. There's this guy talking about loving your neighbour and not casting the first stone unless ye be free of sin, and other, like, really cool stuff. And worshipping only one god.'

'It's the Jews again – don't tell me. Isn't one religion enough for those people? You have *one* religion, with lots of gods.'

'I hate stupid pantheism. It's rubbish.'

'What?! Get one of the slaves to come in here and whack you round the head with a strigil, by Jupiter – and all the others, too numerous to list here.'

'Mum, can I be a Roundhead?'

'No. Put on your two-foot lace collar and fluff your hair out a bit more: it's not nearly wide enough.'

'I know where the priest hole is . . . I-know-where-the-priest-hole-is . . .'

'Right, that's it. I'll give you a priest hole . . .'

'Good night, Mother and Father. God bless the Queen and Prince Albert. Please will you reconsider my wish to go to school?'

'No. Education's for boys. Get back to your attic.'

'Mum, I don't want to be Jewish any more. I've been eating hot dogs garnished with prawns, and I'm pregnant by an unemployed pig farmer called Horst who I've been secretly living with in a derelict Viking longboat off the M62.'

'Well, then get out: you're dead to us. But have this twelve-course snack before you go.'

'Mum, can I be a suicide bomber?'

'No.'

'Why not?! All my friends are.'

'Still no.'

'Thanks for ruining my life!'

(Slam)

I'm sure the single-celled organism that first divided itself was sent to bed early for not toeing the line. Come to think of it, Eve must have been a teenager. You can tell, because decent parents have always blamed the snake.

But without her, where would we be?

Regime Change

'You go.'

'No, you.'

'I don't want them to see me.'

'Oh, *honestly* . . .'

Lawrence is having some friends round for his sixteenth birthday. And having supplied a case of Beck's and some pizzas, we're upstairs in the bedroom, Staying Out of the Way. And I want another gin and tonic while we watch *Dexter*.

When we mentioned this proposed celebration to other parents we were regaled with cautionary tales, each more awful than the last.

The party scene has changed. We hear of fifty – a hundred – gatecrashers; kids with alcohol poisoning found in gardens; the son of the deputy head turning up at the rugby pavilion with a bottle of vodka – and he was only in Year Nine. Several have even made the papers; parties held while parents were away which have ended with eggs and flour thrown at soft furnishings, TVs ripped off walls, doors kicked off hinges and bird baths thrown through windows. And not just round here. A woman rang a radio phone-in programme about it – from Western Australia. There's always a neighbour who says: 'And in such a Nice Area too.'

'So . . .' I say to Lawrence, 'how will you – you know, control the numbers?'

'Firstly, it's a small get-together of about a dozen people, not a rave.'

'Yes, of course.'

'And second, by not being a complete idiot and putting it on Facebook.'

'Ah. Right.'

Peter peers over the banisters and inches down a few steps, like an explorer encountering the territorial markings of a hitherto uncontacted tribe: a discarded fake-fur coat, a pair of muddy black suede platforms and a half-drunk can of something called Venom.

The kitchen is deserted, scattered with half-eaten snacks and blazing with light, like the *Titanic* in its final hour.

He returns with my gin.

'Well?'

'They're all in the garden.'

'What about the pond?'

My Mother Image Bank shows me Rolling Stone Brian Jones, floating face down in his own pool in 1969.

'They're fine. Lawrence is out there.'

As Lawrence himself has lately taken to pointing out:

'I'm not *completely* incompetent: look, here I am putting one foot in front of the other. See?'

So he can probably manage to entertain his friends for a few hours without wrecking the place.

'And it will be tidied *after* my guests have gone. So you don't need to have PTSD because someone's left the tzatziki out – OK, Mother?'

Eventually, all is quiet. Then sometime during the night we hear smashing glass – then humming, and a kind of muffled thumping.

Yet the next day all the mess has gone.

'My God,' says Peter. 'The kitchen is actually *cleaner* than it was.'

'They've even mopped the floor!'

'I think that noise was bottles going into the recycling.'

'And the humming and thumping?'

'Vacuuming. No wonder you didn't recognize it.'

We make coffee, gazing in awe at our spotless surroundings.

What we don't yet realize is that we're witnessing the early signs of regime change. Soon we will be like old royals deposed in a velvet revolution, allowed to stay on in the old palace, but with ceremonial status only.

The new order is a democracy.

Ages 16 & 17: Animal Magic

Time for another hideous extra-curricular experience organized by The School which the kids are supposed to Set Up For Themselves, and which in reality parents end up having to Sort Out At The Last Minute: Year Eleven Work Experience Week.

When it was his turn, Lawrence got a week in the Optical Telecommunications Department at University College London, thanks to my old school-friend Lucy, one of those lovely people who *doesn't* say:

'Gosh, I haven't heard from you for about a year and now you want me to find a job for your child by tomorrow' – because she too is a parent and has Been Through It. And while he didn't come away determined to devote his life to Optical Telecommunications, Lawrence was made a huge fuss of and taken out for pizza. He even helped a bit in the actual lab, though doing what I can't tell you because I didn't understand it.

And now it's Lydia's turn, and she wants to be a vet.

I say:

'Is this like when you were going to be a doctor?'

'What? NO. *God* . . .!'

'Good start,' says Peter. 'Well done.'

She reminds us that she's been interested in animals since at least Year Five, which is true, because I definitely remember having to watch *Animal Emergency*. Then, more recently, she became devoted to the *Supervet*. And in between there were the guinea pigs, the sweet but agoraphobic members of the household who failed to enhance our lives in any way, though she did usually clean out their cage.

'Well then!'

But you have to get A-star in about twenty subjects, because getting in to do Veterinary Science is harder even than Medicine – harder than becoming Pope, by the look of it – though I don't understand why.

'Because unlike doctors, you have to know all the anatomy for every kind of animal, instead of just one,' says Lydia, none too patiently.

Blimey.

But how can she get any Work Experience? We don't know any vets.

'Hang on,' says Peter. 'I'm having an idea . . .'

His friend Jonathan is now a writer but used to be a farmer, having swapped one impossible way to make a living for another.

'He's bound to know a vet.'

And he does. Not only that, but Lydia can stay with him, his wife and two little girls, near Totnes where the vet is based. Work experience *and* a week in her beloved Devon countryside. Solved!

She gets the train down and is taken to the vet's each day by Jonathan's wife Jess – because in the country you have to drive everywhere – and reads bedtime stories to the two lovely little girls in the evenings, and it all sounds idyllic.

She returns, having attended a neutering and a canine mastectomy, and a bovine ante-natal session at one of the local farms.

'Did the Bernese mountain dog mind being "done"?' I say.

'He was *unconscious*.'

'What did you do?'

'Just watched.'

'Right. And did you get to feel any of the calf embryos?'

'No! I just wrote down which cows were pregnant.'

'OK. So how do you feel about becoming a vet?'

She looks appalled.

'Absolutely *no way* am I doing that.'

'Oh. Why not?'

'I was on my feet ALL DAY.'

Still, her interest in animals undimmed, she and I go to the cinema to see *Rams*, a darkly humorous Icelandic drama about two feuding brothers, both sheep farmers, and the unexpected events that force their relationship to change.

'Lydia must be the only teenage girl in Britain,' observes Peter, 'who actively wants to see a film about Icelandic sheep farmers.'

The film is good: tense, poignant and punctuated by deadpan humour. And all goes well until about halfway through, when a trio of teenage boys come in through the fire exit. They talk loudly and play with their phones, making no attempt to keep their voices down, until eventually it's so distracting I say, politely but firmly:

'If you're not going to watch the film, could you please go out?'

And, with a bit of muttering and hissing, they do. I hold my breath for a few moments, as they pass us. Then, slightly to my surprise, instead of telling me off for being embarrassing, Lydia leans over and says:

'Thank you for doing that.'

When we come out into the foyer, she sees the same boys sitting at a table, and we point them out to the staff, mentioning their behaviour, the fact that they almost certainly came in without paying – and their blatant lack of appreciation for contemporary Scandinavian cinema.

'I suppose they were harmless enough,' I say, 'but it was *so annoying*.'

And Lydia says:

'For one crazy moment I thought they might lock the doors and start shooting.'

What?

But it's not so crazy, is it?

It's only three months since the horrific killings in Paris. And America has had two recent shootings in cinemas, in 2012 and last year. So people have actually been murdered while watching movies. The cinema, my favourite place, is no longer inviolable. I don't think for a minute Lydia will stop going, but I want to say something – useful. Yet none of the words that come to mind seem up to the job.

Outside, Brixton is its usual self. There's steel pan music drifting over from near the tube station, mingled with entreaties from a man outside KFC to invite the Eternal Lord Jesus into our lives.

We walk to the bus stop.

'Aside from those idiots interrupting,' I say, 'what did you think of the film?'

'Good: I liked it.'

The bus comes and we get on.

And as it pulls away, the Voice that announces the stops has a new message for us.

'Please hold on,' it says, 'while the bus is moving.'

'Phew,' says Lydia. 'Because we wouldn't want to fall over, would we?'

Ages 17 & 18:
Au Revoir and Toodle-Pip

In the autumn, Lawrence will be going to university – in Manchester, two hundred miles away. It's really happening!

He'll be only just eighteen. But it's not purely about the degree.

'No offence. But I really want to get away.'

Oh.

Thanks.

But I know he's right.

It's just going to be such a wrench. I never left home, or went to university; the whole idea is utterly alien.

What's it like? How does it feel?

I ask our friend Sarah H how it felt when her girls went off.

'It was really hard during the first year,' she says, 'when they'd come home, dump their bags and go off with their new friends.'

Gulp! The dreaded tumble turn.

I just know I'll be standing at the door with a freshly baked cake and a DVD of *21 Jump Street*, looking totally desperate.

As he heads towards the end of his last ever year at school, I distract myself from the coming Exodus by collecting recipes from the papers that I think look tempting and relatively achievable, and sending optimistic texts like:

How abt mkg spag bol with me later? – in the breezy tone of someone who's just spontaneously come up with the idea and hasn't been thinking about it for days. And who isn't his mother.

And I either get no response, or:

Bit busy now, maybe later.

'He's taking his A levels,' says Peter. 'Leave it.'

'But the A levels are finished now.'

'Then he's winding down after all that hard work. Leave it: he'll be fine.'

'But he's going to be Out There,' I say. 'Unable to cook.'

I am gripped by the fear that he'll live on alcohol, takeaways coated in mysterious blends of spices and antibiotics, and food-like, chemical compounds in packets. And by the end of the first year, my healthy glowing lad will be reduced to a hollow-eyed stick.

Or worse, a lump of grey flab. He might as well be saying: 'I'm leaving home specifically in order to eat rubbish and ruin my health.'

'But no one in your family ever learned to cook before leaving home,' says Peter. 'And look at you now. And your sister.'

True. I only really got interested in it when the children were small, to avoid putting them to bed. I can put plain chicken pieces on a tray with a few veg and get praised for it, like the Emperor's New Supper.

'So,' he says, 'I think you should calm down and stop worrying. It's actually getting a bit tiresome.'

'OK,' I say. 'No more about Lawrence and food.'

And as soon as he's out of the way I get out the special scrapbook I've been saving for Lawrence's New Life, with pages for copying and pasting in recipes, and little integral folders for tucking in the ones cut out of magazines.

I start with my lazy tortilla, basically a big omelette filled with anything you find in the fridge and not folded, because it's like trying to fold a mattress, but finished under the grill.

Then I put in my dad's braised lamb, the first meal he made me at his flat when I was five, using ultra-cheap middle neck of lamb, onions, potatoes and carrots like Irish Stew, but also – since he wasn't Irish – tinned tomatoes. I also include dual-purpose meatballs – press down to make burgers – and basic tomato sauce. And gravy. I find it hard to leave things out, so he ends up with about twenty of my own favourites, plus quite a lot of others I've saved over the years. Then I cover the whole thing with a luscious picture of pancakes with blueberries and cream, cut out of the *Observer Food Magazine*.

Then I move onto Life Tips, such as How to Prevent Hangovers, How to Avoid Getting into a Fight – always, *always* back down – and How to Stay out of Debt, though with this I've reckoned without the government raising the future interest on student loans to over 6 per cent. So I just say Not to Buy Anything Involving a Purchase Plan, since 'A top of the range motor for £200 a month!' usually means £200 a month for four thousand years at 1,000 per cent APR. Finally I add How to Wash Up, since, being the Dishwasher Generation, they've hardly ever done any, and I'm married to someone who never uses enough washing-up liquid, which might be genetic.

And I know that I've been imagining him – and his sister – as empty vessels, waiting, like jugs on a shelf, for knowledge to be poured in, forgetting that the main point of *going* to university is to find these things out for yourself. And that even if you don't, as I didn't, you find out stuff anyway – just by living. But I do it all the same.

The packing begins, and seems to go on for days. On the day he's due to leave, I go into his room and put the scrapbook on his bed, near the two boxes of spare pans, mixing bowls, wooden spoons, a whisk, a potato masher and several food canisters I've saved.

Then he comes in and says:

'Can you not put things on the bed? I'm laying all my stuff out there.'

So I move it close to one of his holdalls, without actually putting it in. But it's in the way, so I put it on top of one of the boxes of kitchen utensils. And he looks up and says:

'You know I won't be using all this, right?'

As if I've packed five sleeping bags, two tents and a harpoon.

'You're not going catered, so you will have to *eat*.'

'Can you just let me *pack*?'

'Why not just take the cutlery and a couple of pans,' I concede eventually. 'Just in case.'

And he puts down his beer, reverts to his serious face – the one I imagine he'll use to tell us he's been caught dealing at a festival or got someone pregnant – and says:

273

'Mum, this fantasy of yours, of me cooking for my friends all gathered round the table, just Isn't Going to Happen.'

And I say:

'I know.'

And I carry on collecting recipes because parents aren't as intelligent as laboratory rats and don't learn.

For his Last Supper I make paella, which I learned from Pablo, a small hotel owner – or owner of a small hotel – near Ronda some years back.

On The Day, which is unusually warm for September, Lawrence puts on shorts and flip-flops, which make him look more vulnerable.

And suddenly it's Time.

And Lydia and I go out to the stuffed car for a final hug. And Peter says he's just going to back it out, and runs over Lawrence's foot.

'PETER!'

'DAD!'

'*DA-AD!!*'

'Go back! *Go back*!'

And Peter goes back, and somehow manages to run over his foot *again*.

And I rush forward, the whole scenario – A&E, X-rays, crutches, the missed freshers' week – all flashing across my head like a running news caption.

'Oh my God!'

And Peter gets out of the car and says,

'Are you all right?! I am *so, so sorry*.'

And Lawrence lifts up his foot, looks at it, and says,

'I'm OK: it's fine.'

Maybe we've just witnessed a circus trick, that we – and he – didn't know he could do. Or could it be a message from the universe saying: Your Child is Stronger than You Think? Literally, as the children like to say, and metaphorically.

And he gives Lydia a huge hug, and me a huge hug, pressing my head against his reassuringly solid chest.

And then they're gone.

Lydia and I get fish and chips and watch *A Knight's Tale*, the film for every occasion, especially when your firstborn has left to make his way in the world and become a self-non-catering student.

'Lawrence could be William Thatcher,' she says.

'And you're definitely the beautiful farting blacksmith.'

Certainly not the soppy princess.

'It'll be all right,' she says, and strokes my hair. 'Did he take the utensils in the end?'

'I'm slightly avoiding going in his room, so I'm not sure.'

He won't be cooking, I accept that now.

And before I go to bed on that first night, and for the next few nights, I do walk quickly past his door, in case I find myself sitting on his bed and breathing in the smell of one of his jumpers, as people do in dramas when someone has been killed.

'I feel OK,' I say. 'In fact, I think I can get through this.'

'That's good,' she says, looking relieved.

'Just as long as *you* never leave.'

'Ha ha!'

'No, really.'

You'd think evolution would have come up with something less emotionally draining. Couldn't they just pack a bag, salute and say:

'Well, Mother – I suppose it's au revoir and toodle-pip.'

And couldn't we just smile brightly and reply:

'Goodbye, darling. And – good luck!'

A few days in, I get my first text from the Other Side:

What do you advise, for my first food shop?

And I feel like a woman in an old Hollywood epic, hearing that her son has found the One True Faith.

I dash off a random list of staples – *rice, onions,*

noodles, tinned toms, beans, cheap jar olives? – before he changes his mind and asks someone else.

Then, a few weeks into the term, a breathless text arrives, in the same tone as I imagine that of Victorian explorers when they first beheld the Pyramids:

Big Asian shop has 12 tins of toms for £2.40!!

Followed a few days later by:

Just made huge pan of dahl. So cheap!

A month later I get:

Dinner tonight. Veggie chilli con carne with chickpeas, sour cream, tarragon and mint dip.

Wow. You cooking for others too?

Sometimes eat with others, sometimes make lots and keep portions.

The shock of my child actually doing this thing I wanted is thrilling but a bit unnerving. I feel like someone who's nagged their child to practise *Ten Little Fingers*, only to see them pull out a guitar and start working their way through the repertoire of Prince.

By the end of term he's made chicken tikka masala from scratch with his new flatmate Jack, lemon-marinated pesto chicken with paprika chilli sweet potato chips and garlic yogurt dip, and for their Christmas dinner, roast-chicken-with-everything for ten. I get a last-minute text about roast potatoes, but by the time I've replied *parboil & shake in pan to make crispy edges* he's gone ahead and fed the whole flat.

In December he comes back for the holidays, and I make what may well be my last Christmas lunch.

'I'm about to be redundant.'

'Let's not get carried away,' he says. 'You still have your uses.'

'The washing up, no doubt!'

'Show me how you do gravy,' he says, to soften the blow of my impending obsolescence.

The last few meals he makes before he goes back in January are tinged with an unsettling sensation, of longing mixed with dread. When I see him cutting a lemon on the counter without a board, I'm just about to warn him not to scratch it when he rolls the lemon under the knife, cutting only the upper surface to spare the worktop. And I feel a kind of wrenching, like my friend Steve's description of his mother's last kiss before the train used to pull away to take him to boarding school: the overwhelming intensity of the love, combined with something very like grief.

'He misses you too, you know,' Peter explains.

'Really?'

'Of course! What do you think?!'

'I don't know. I have no sense of it.'

I'm aware it's one of these things most people take

as read, but that I have to be taught, like people with no nerve endings having to be reminded that hot things burn.

Once he goes back I resume texting him for cooking tips.

Maybe give up Maths and open restnt?

Ha, maybe.

Btw did u find anything useful in the scrapbook?

Going to get round to it, yeh yeh.

But it takes me a long time to actually call him. I fear he might not want to hear from me and will cut me off early to go and do something more interesting. It feels far too like the early weeks of a new relationship. Perhaps in a way it is.

Baby Come Back

Like a wave depositing fleeces, old flip-flops and about a dozen carrier bags through the hall, Lawrence returns.

This time he looks completely different; his hair is very short, and he seems to be growing a beard.

He clasps Lydia to him, his head clearly visible above hers, and swivels her slightly back and forth. I step forward.

And he walks past me.

I've been practising – or if not quite *practising*, reminding myself not to be too *intense*. And anyhow, I don't want to come over like someone who's been waiting all these weeks, with nothing else to do.

So, don't be intense, don't sound desperate, don't start a complicated conversation right away. 'Can I come into the house first?' I seem to remember him saying when he once came back from a holiday with his friends.

And don't *cry*.

And this is particularly hard because when he left at the end of the last holidays, I drove him to the tube station with his new girlfriend, and they both sat in the back, looking at something on his phone the whole time. And when I pulled over – there's nowhere to stop, so you do have to fling the door open like a getaway driver – they got out and just walked away. Didn't say goodbye, thank you for the lift, nothing.

I drove home, trying to talk myself out of a massive overreaction. *He does love you, come on, you know he does.* And feeling absolutely bereft.

Did my mother miss me when I first went to Dad's on Fridays? She never said so, never went for a last hug as I dragged my heels on the stairs. But maybe she did.

I say:

'Would you like a drink?'

OMG! I can't believe you just did that.

'Are you hungry?'

You didn't even look at me.

'How about outside? The garden's really nice at the moment.'

I give Peter a look. He gives me his 'FFS rise above it'.

I wasn't desperate, I wasn't intense. I'm being Casual! PLEASE HUG ME!

Sarah H said: 'It was awful when they used to dump their bags and go off with their friends.'

Other people have this too. That helps, right?

No: it doesn't.

But he doesn't go off with his friends. He opens a beer, leans against the counter, encloses me in a manly yet filial hug, and says:

'So, Mother: what shall I make for supper?'

Last Exit to Westworld

Lawrence is down for the summer, and on a sunny day in July we drive to Kent, to take my mother to lunch at the village pub. Conversationally, she has slowed down. What hasn't changed is that she still doesn't ask the children about themselves.

'Why not ask them what *they're* doing?' I snap.

All my encounters with her come loaded with the baggage of many volatile years, like the history of a lovely but troubled island. Whereas the children are only on holiday at this apparently marvellous granny, I'm the returning native unable to forget the battles and demonstrations of the past. As tourists here, they only see the beach.

Afterwards Peter and Lawrence walk behind her as she moves along, inch by inch, bent over her walker. She cannot balance anymore and has no feeling in her feet. Lydia and I go ahead, to put the kettle on – and because I can't bear to watch my once tall, beautiful mother taking such tiny, panicky steps.

The path is narrow, with next-door's wall on one side, and her tall garden boundary on the other. Just a few yards from the house, she comes to a stop. As she anxiously grips the handles of the walker – and the brakes – Peter and Lawrence are trapped behind her in the gateway. None of them can move.

We don't know there's anything wrong until we hear them calling from the front garden.

'Cushions!' they shout. 'Get some cushions!'

We rush out to see them straining to hold her upright as her legs fold slowly beneath her until she is stuck in a kneeling position on the path, her knees splayed painfully outwards. Behind her, still jammed in the gateway, Peter and Lawrence can't lift her; they're going to try to break her fall, which seems to happen in slow motion.

Lydia and I run back and forth with about a dozen cushions – some beautifully decorated by Mum with her fabric paints – and pass them over her head and they try to wedge them under her to stop her folding up like a broken chair.

It's no use. She's in pain and can't move.

I dial 999.

Within minutes two burly paramedics appear, and with no chance of getting through the blocked gateway, somehow prise my mother's hands off the walker, release Peter and Lawrence back along the path, and extricate her. Then they effortlessly lift her into the ambulance and whisk her away.

'No need to follow,' I tell Peter. 'It'll be an X-ray at most, then she'll be back.'

I have no idea that we're on the approach to our final separation.

Later I learn she has fractured her 'tib-and-fib' – tibia and fibula, the two major bones in the lower leg. When I get there the next day, the break has been set, but within a few hours she has lost her normally healthy appetite, causing her digestive system to break down. And the little mobility she had is now gone.

The hospital visits over the next seven, terrible weeks are so stressful, the doctors so elusive, the communication so appalling and the expectations for an elderly patient so incredibly low, that I come back trembling with anger and despair. My sister, who alternates with me, brings mum her favourite snacks: apricots, olives and avocados with little pots of home-made vinaigrette, all of which are barely touched.

When I bring Lawrence, he shows her an episode of *Mock the Week* on his phone. She laughs, though I sense the pace is now too fast for her. We beg her to eat an apricot, or an olive. How about some avocado, with Claire's delicious dressing? She has one mouthful. Tea, coffee and water all sit mostly untouched.

'If you eat and drink, Mum, you'll be able to get out of here.'

It's like a distorted mirror of Lawrence's first meal as a baby.

This is what a really badly run institution is like, where people actually do die in corridors, and what many of us have to look forward to. Never mind Oxbridge and learning Mandarin: we need to know how to survive *this*.

Lawrence comes away shaking his head in bewilderment, and we go to a nearby pub. After two hours' begging her to eat, and pleading with the staff to recognize that she is fading away, I can't even summon the words 'gin and tonic', so he sends me to the garden to sit down.

'What did you choose?' I say.

'A Bloody Mary. I did have to tell them how to make it, though.'

Maybe the barman moonlights at the hospital.

'See what I've been going on about?'

'Mothership,' he says, 'you did not exaggerate.'

'Fuck fuck *fuck*!'

'There there.'

'I can't stand it!'

'Sssh, ssh, it'll be OK.'

It won't, of course, but hearing him say it is unexpectedly reassuring in a way it wouldn't be coming from another adult, such as the distant cousin who replies to my email that Mum is deteriorating with a breezy 'Chin up!'

When you waddle into the delivery suite, or your home birthing spa or wherever, you're not having a baby: you're having someone to comfort you when your own parent is dying.

While we're worrying about trivia like whether they're top in Chemistry or going to be picked for the football team, our children are not only getting better at doing stuff, like eating their vegetables and packing something other than cuddly toys to take on holiday, they're developing compassion and leadership skills. Maybe they already have the compassion, then learn to deploy it on their own parents.

Now I see why in some societies they have a lot of children: one to get the drinks; one to queue for food because suddenly cooking is too overwhelming; one to go upstairs and squeeze between the filing cabinet and the wall in the study to reset the Wi-Fi booster which is plugged into the hardest to reach socket in the house. And one to look up the Mental Capacity Act 2005, for ammunition should we need it, when we realize she isn't going to come out, and – even if it means a fight – we're going to get her out of there so her last days on earth will be spent somewhere less like hell.

Yet to have that golden hour in the sunny pub garden, with him, nearly makes the whole horrible experience worth it.

'I could stand almost anything,' I say, 'just to have a drink among the flowers with you.'

'Mother,' he says. 'You really do need to get out more.'

'When you finish university,' I say, 'come home and never leave.'

He puts his arm round me.

If either of us is ever dropped into a catastrophe like this, will he and his sister get us out?

Eventually we track down a nice geriatric specialist, hidden at the end of an unmarked corridor – possibly to prevent any elderly patients finding him – and in late September, he gets my mother moved to an excellent local care home. And because she won't be there very long, and he does the secret form no one knows about, it's free.

Lawrence and Lydia come and arrange family drawings and photos on the wall by her bed, chatting casually as if they do this all the time.

'Granny, look – I'm putting the bird picture there.'

'And the photo of us over here.'

'You're facing the garden and there are bird feeders!'

I put up a copy of an engraving from a Victorian obstetric manual that she likes, of a doctor reaching under a woman's ankle-length skirt, captioned: *'You should be able to get Freeview now.'*

The people there are lovely and she lasts another three and a half weeks, pretty good going for someone whose last full meal was in July.

At the beginning of October, a care assistant rings me sounding agitated, but I can't understand what she's saying, thanks to a very strong South-East Asian accent. Plus she's using a term I don't know.

'She's what? I don't understand.'

It sounds like 'sy-no'.

What the fuck is *sy-no*?

'Can you spell it? Spell it, please!'

It's *cyanosed*.

Lydia grabs a phone and looks it up.

'It means she's gone blue.'

Oh. Nice image. Thanks.

Lawrence is back in Manchester and my sister has hurt her back, so it's just us.

'Can you come soon?' the woman adds bluntly. 'She's near the end.'

We pack quickly.

'Is that your toothbrush?'

'Lydia, hurry up!'

'My mother's dying . . . Fucking hell!'

'Are you all right, Mum?'

'Mm. I just feel really weird. Should I bring my boots?'

'What? Why?'

'In case we go for a walk.'

There's a particularly good walk, from her front door. You walk through the village and past the allotments, where the children used to pick her raspberries – carefully avoiding the huge beds of chard – then you climb steeply up onto the North Downs Way, stop by the chalk crown – like a white horse, but a crown, and gaze down at the village below. We'll be staying at the house; a walk might be just the thing.

We get down the M20 without speeding, and miss The End by fifteen minutes.

The staff stayed with her and held her hand. That's somehow the saddest part. I still don't know why people being nice makes you cry.

'You don't have to come in and see her,' I tell Lydia.

So she goes into the lounge, where she's shown to a row of chairs, arranged as if in an airport or on a ferry, and given a mug of tea.

I've seen a dead body before, I tell myself: I'm no longer a corpse virgin. And it can't be as hard as seeing my father, who died with no warning at all.

She's lying on her back, her skin stretched over her cheekbones, almost as if she's had a face-lift – not her style, as she was never vain. And her mouth is slightly open, suggesting disconcertingly that she might be about to speak. There's also a breathing sound, which is really, really –

'What IS that? Peter, don't leave!'

'I think it's the special mattress.'

The staff are very kind, but they do want the name of an undertaker quite soon. So I come back out to borrow Lydia's phone charger; we don't want the phone dying as well.

'Here you are,' she says. 'And Mum – look at this.'

She holds up her tea: the mug is captioned 'LOL!' and below that, so you really can't avoid it: 'Laugh Out Loud.'

'Granny would have appreciated it, don't you think?'

I do.

Part of her so clearly comes from my mother, and

291

– which seems even more counterintuitive – part of what we've got right as parents is from her too. Even as I have consciously Not Done What My Parents Did, I have been drawing on their contribution. In fact, even the Not Doing What Your Parents Did might be something I've learned from them too.

'D'you think it's OK to laugh, though?' she says.

'Oh yes.'

Peter finds us a friendly undertaker and I haggle a bit over the willow casket, then we go back to the house, get a Chinese takeaway and watch the first episode of the new *Westworld* on our iPad. It's based on the film she took me to when it came out in 1973, one of her absolute favourites. We both fancied Yul Brynner, even as a murderous cowboy android.

Lydia says:

'It's literally what Granny would have wanted.'

It is.

And she would have appreciated her grandchild supplying the punchline.

Xenomorph

Late last night, when the four of us got back from seeing *Alien Covenant*, Peter poured me a Scotch to soothe me after the sight of yet another crew kebabbed in their own ship.

Instead of being hunched down in her seat, terrified, like me, my daughter was scrutinizing the hardware and the latest incarnations of the Xenomorph, studying minute changes in the detail. When you speculate about which family traits are inherited, you somehow don't imagine this.

My mother told me once that her fascination with insects mitigated any anxiety. Where others saw a threat, she marvelled at the science. The day we had to run unexpectedly from a swarm of bees in Dad's garden, she actually walked, quite calmly, gazing up at them in admiration, while he and I legged it into the house.

And I do think that if the bees or ants had got into power during her lifetime she would have worked for them quite willingly. She might even have stood, mesmerized, in front of a ravenous, glistening Neomorph, as the synthetic David does in *Covenant*, though I know she would never have sacrificed us humans. Well, I'm pretty sure she wouldn't, though she did believe that ants and bees both had a superior social structure.

I once bought Lydia *The World of H.R. Giger*, a book of drawings by the Swiss chappie who designed the Xenomorph for the original film – but I was in a hurry, so only glanced at it.

The night before her tenth birthday when I got it out to wrap it, I had a quick flick through. Along with the first sketches for *Alien* and other variations on that theme, were some similar creatures having very obvious sex with human women – I mean, not at all subtle or discreet. And they were quite, well, phallically challenging – though not *challenged*.

So I shoved it back again, on the Present Shelf with the spare books, novelty socks, periodic table tea towels, and DVDs; I have three of *Shakespeare in Love*, my go-to gift when stuck. I also taped the phallic pages together just in case it was discovered by a visiting toddler – or worse, their parents.

Eventually, of course, she found it, though by then she was a good few years older – about fourteen. And

I still didn't intend giving it to her; even if she didn't freak out, I assumed she'd have to hide it from her friends.

'Hey, Lyds, what did you get for Christmas?'

'Oh, a pair of jeans, some bubble bath, a set of wolf coasters and a book of huge, psychotic homicidal arthropods, some of them having sex with women.'

'Oh . . .'

So I explained that I'd bought it after only the most minimal scrutiny, and only later discovered the sci-fi porn. She untaped the pages, looked through it without reacting and said:

'I see what you mean! But the designs are so cool. Can I have it?'

All right, I thought. *No one's crying; it's not rape.* I thought I might even spin it the other way, if I found myself in the company of anyone really uptight.

'And oh my God, when she opened it on her tenth birthday, along with the Lego and friendship bracelet set . . .!'

That'd take their minds off the catastrophe of their child getting a B.

Then it was Hallowe'en and she bought a dark blue leotard, which she dyed black, and a little French knitting device, to make the narrow 'cable-y' things that go round the Alien's chest, and spent several hours shaping some papier mâché on an armature – made from some of my anti-squirrel wire – to make the disturbingly long head, edged with teeth. Then she devoted a further few hours to the inner jaw, with a delicate criss-cross mechanism like you see on those novelty boxing gloves that spring out at you. But in this case, being inside the head, it only came out when bitten down on at the back, which was excellent though quite uncomfortable, and no homework was done for the whole weekend. And once it was on, she couldn't really *see*.

But she was led around the area by her friends for about forty minutes, then came back for hot chocolate, having scared a satisfying number of the locals. And the head lived on the kitchen radiator for a while, causing guests to glance uncomfortably in its direction between sips of wine or tea, before asking,

'What *is* that?'

'Why don't you do something with the Alien Head?' I'd say from time to time, the way women say to their husbands, 'Why don't you do something with that pile of wood in the garage?' and she'd look at me blankly – because, as I eventually realized, the process of making it was the exciting part.

And so now, as I sip my whisky, I see that intense concentration again, as she lines up her ruler on a squared pad and starts to draw.

'What are you designing?'

'A bed. They're all too expensive, so I've decided to make one.'

She has a boyfriend now, so a larger bed makes sense. Anyhow, I'm Not Drawing Attention to it. She liked him from the off because he once made his own wolf costume, *and* he has a film degree so I can now mention François Truffaut to someone who doesn't roll their eyes.

And I think that deciding to make her first bed after seeing an *Alien* film might make a great anecdote for *The Graham Norton Show*:

'And so, Lydia . . .! How did you first get the inspiration for your – I have to say *un-uuu-sual* furniture designs?'

Cut to still of extraordinary bed, commissioned for someone like Tim Burton or Lady Gaga: trademark ironic look to camera. Audience laughter.

'Well, Graham! I'd just been to see *Alien: Covenant* with my family . . .'

For a moment I'm lost in the reverie. Then I remember the actual design is sitting in front of me.

'Hey,' I say. 'Show me.'

She unfolds the graph paper, and I can't stop myself from saying:

'Oh!'

And she says,
'What?'
'No, no – it's great.'

To my absolute amazement, it's rectangular, with dovetailed corners, and no weird headboard of any kind: a completely normal bed.

With her you just never know *what* to expect.

At the weekend we're in the garden, Lydia assembling our new barbecue set, when we have another arthropod encounter: with a stag beetle, our first in ages. It's been so long I'd forgotten we ever had them.

'It's a female,' she says.

They're smaller than the males, with smaller antlers, but still pretty big.

Up close they look huge, as if on steroids, and when flying as if too heavy to stay in the air. The larvae feed on decaying wood, which makes them the ideal offspring, although thanks to the decline in the amount of woodland and 'untidy' open spaces they're now endangered. Also, people kill them because they 'look frightening'. No wonder I feel a bond.

Lydia watches closely.

The beetle strides boldly across the patio, starts to climb up the back wall of the house – an acrobatic sort of female, a bit like Lydia. But she falls off, onto her back.

'Turn her over!'

I can't bear to see her struggling.

But Lydia says,

'No, she can do it.'

I'm itching to right the frantically waggling creature, but Lydia holds me back.

'I believe in you!' she chants, relishing my frustration.

After what seems a long time but is probably only about six seconds, the beetle wiggles herself back onto her front and ambles off into the undergrowth. And Lydia resumes screwing together the barbecue, fixing me with a knowing look.

'Don't say it,' I say.

'I'm not!'

And she doesn't.

Play 'Beetroot' for Me

I get out my old ghetto-blaster and put in the first tape I made for the car when the kids were small.

'Aaah! Remember this?'

It's 'Mrs Robinson', from *The Graduate*, and although we haven't played it for ages, Peter and I both remember exactly what comes next: 'California Dreaming', then 'The Age of Aquarius' and 'Let the Sunshine In'. Then: '24 Hours from Tulsa', 'Trains & Boats & Planes', 'Walk On By', 'The James Bond Theme' and 'Raindrops Keep Fallin' on my Head', from the only soppy scene in *Butch Cassidy and the Sundance Kid*. I don't know why, when we both forget a whole load of important things pretty much daily, the songs on our old cassettes are fixed in our heads, in the right order, forever. No wonder music is the last thing to go; I can see us one day in our care home, shouting,

'No, no, next should be "White Rabbit"!' as we're injected with something nice and calming for the sake of the other residents.

I can remember my dad getting the Simon and Garfunkel LP with 'Mrs Robinson' on it when it came out, and my mother coming back from seeing *Hair* when it opened here, the same year, elated from having got up with half the audience and danced onstage. She could sing the whole soundtrack, if you didn't stop her.

I made this tape for Lydia and Lawrence when they were three and four, with a selection not just of my own taste, but tracks that as children they could easily latch on to and remember. And to avoid the theme songs from the likes of *Bob the Builder* – which got to number one the year Lawrence turned four and was therefore quite hard to escape. To the question, 'Can we fix it?' one could only reply: 'Yes, but only by closing all the windows to blot out the radios of passing traffic and hurling the VHS into the pond.'

Car journeys became enjoyable. They loved the pop classics and quickly chose their own favourites.

'Play "Beetroot".'

'What's that, darling?'

'"Beetroot"! YOU KNOW!'

They went on and on asking – with increasing frustration – for this song that neither of us could recall ever having heard. Eventually it came round on the tape and they cried,

'THAT's it! Why did you say we didn't *have* it?!'

It was in fact 'Be True to Yourself' sung by Bobby Vee.

And thus the whole tape was renamed 'Beetroot', with the next one, of a similarly eclectic range, 'New Beetroot'.

Then, because she too is a bit nostalgic, Lydia loads the contents of both Beetroots onto the iPod for us, and on the way back from a trip out of town Peter and I play the whole thing.

Then a track comes on I'd forgotten was on there.

'Not an *obvious* choice on a tape for children,' says Peter somewhat disapprovingly, and I listen as Donna Summer's multi-orgasmic disco anthem 'Love to Love You Baby' issues from the vehicle's pretty powerful speakers – the kind that turn the heads of passing police patrols, or would if we weren't white.

'This was *your* choice,' I say. 'I only included it so there'd be Something For Everyone: along with The Beatles, *Hair*, and all that West Coast hippy stuff you like.'

'And that the children also do like.'

I avoid bringing up the menu of sexual practices we discovered on the *Hair* soundtrack album that Lydia would announce with:

'This is the one you have to skip over, Mummy,' during a phase of being demure she went through for about a week.

'All right. Whatever. The point is you chose it, so its unsuitability or whatever is your fault not mine.'

The Donna Summer smash was unfortunately never the same for me after it was played repeatedly at the hotel in Tunisia where I went on holiday with my friend Claudia and her mother the summer after it came out. The creepy MC who controlled the turntable would talk along with the lyrics in a dire monotone – not to mention a way too tight, traditionally embroidered waistcoat: imagine Edina from *Ab Fab* but with stubble – *every single time*.

'Lurve-ta lurve-ya, bebeh . . .'

Forty years on, I still can't quite shake it free of his sleazy growl.

Peter is frowning at Donna's mounting excitement issuing from the speakers in the front, back and both door panels, as we crawl through the fringes of South London.

'How old were they, though?' he says. 'About four? Five, tops.'

'There's nothing wrong with children seeing sex as a positive thing,' I say. 'And besides, at that age they wouldn't even have noticed what it was about.'

'What, they just thought it was a recording of a woman moving a wardrobe?'

'Hilarious. As I say, not my fault.'

Just then the traffic slows right down, and as we grind to a halt, windows open, the sound of that really quite convincing climax – where all the music stops and it's just her, breathing – booms out clearly to the car in the next lane. No one looks round.

'Ah, well that's Croydon for you,' he says.

At least on this occasion the children aren't there; they have lately begun to ruin our happy reminiscences with self-righteous complaints about our alleged failure to provide age-appropriate entertainment when they were younger.

This issue next rears its head over supper one night before Lawrence goes back to Manchester, when the conversation turns to curious phrases and sayings.

'*Talk to the Hand*,' I say, recalling the title of the Lynne Truss book. 'I suppose that's gone now, because of *Game of Thrones* and the Hand of the King. Because, you know, people really do talk to the Hand.'

'Anyway it's Queen now.'

'All *right*.'

'Or "gun of the hand" in *Witness*,' adds Peter. 'When the Amish dad talks about Harrison Ford's revolver.'

'Yeah!' says Lawrence.

'Ah . . . *Witness*,' says Peter. 'We must watch that again at Christmas.'

Although it's only August we're already compiling our list. Last year we watched four films on 25 December, the upside of having almost no relatives.

Then Lydia says:

'That's the one where the guy has a bag put over his head and gets his throat cut.'

'What?' I say. 'I think *most* people remember it as the film in which Harrison Ford doesn't sleep with Kelly McGillis and it's unbearably romantic.'

'Yeah, well *I* remember the guy having his throat cut. In the railway station toilets.'

For some reason this detail has slipped my mind.

'We were only, like, eight when you made us watch it.'

'We didn't "make you watch it". *God* . . .'

'You were *always* showing us things too young,' Lawrence chimes in.

'No, we weren't. And you definitely weren't *eight*. More like twelve.'

'We were no way *twelve*!'

Peter and I look at each other: are we the only people in Britain whose children wish their viewing had been more *bland*? I know *Saturday Night Fever* was a mistake. And *Spartacus*: Lawrence was definitely too young for crucifixion. But I've apologized for those. Yet here we are again, as if in front of some kind of tribunal.

'What about when you watched *Fifty Sexiest Pop Videos*?' I ask Lydia, 'when you were about *nine*?'

'That doesn't count. Anyhow, it was my choice, so obviously not the same thing.'

'They're worse than my dad,' says Peter. 'Actually, wait – come to think of it, he took me to see *A Clockwork Orange*.'

That was X-rated, i.e. 18+, and considered *so* violent that Anthony Burgess, the writer of the original book, campaigned successfully to have it withdrawn.

'Your father really took you to see it?'

I remember mine shuddering at the posters.

But now I think about it, both my parents showed me quite a lot of films and TV dramas that were rather – shall we say, *sophisticated* – for a child.

Once, the TV was on, showing the trial of some captured Nazi doctors, with testimony from survivors they'd experimented on. And my mother, who had several Jewish friends – not to mention her ex, my father – didn't want to miss any of it by attempting to send me to bed, because the inevitable pleading to stay up would interrupt her viewing.

So aged about nine or ten I found myself watching

that, and, round at my father's, Ingmar Bergman's *Persona*, which contains news footage of the monk who set himself on fire to protest against the Vietnam War. Oh yes, and in the same film, a hand with a nail being banged into it, although at least that was faked. I think.

'I saw all sorts of "unsuitable" films when I was young,' I tell Lawrence and Lydia firmly. 'And it was FINE.'

The weird thing is, it was.

But if anything changes, and I become a Nazi doctor or start setting fire to any clerics, tempted though I am from time to time – I'll get back to you.

Pier Group

What *really* influences people's behaviour?

I go to a talk by a leading scientist on the Teenage Brain and learn, among other things, that young male drivers have more accidents when their friends are in the car. Well – *duh!*

In the talk, peer pressure comes up a lot. In my day, if someone went off the rails her parents usually blamed her friends, and I bet that hasn't changed. But are teenagers genuinely more suggestible, more likely to copy each other than adults are?

True, Lydia and some of her friends did all suddenly dye their hair two-tone recently, in a brief trend that left them with a lovely rich auburn on top – and peroxide blonde underneath. To ensure the full impact wasn't lost on the teaching staff, Lydia put hers in a ponytail to expose the bleached bit, leading to a firmly worded call from the Head of Middle School, who after a grovelling apology from me, conceded that at least it would soon wash out.

'Um, it's semi-permanent,' I mumbled, 'But I wasn't there when it was done. I was – away.'

But that wasn't peer pressure – it was fashion, though on the same spectrum.

No, I know what the scientist meant: young people do reckless things sometimes because their friends do, or to play to the crowd. What, and adults don't?

What this world view also doesn't allow for is their emotional awareness, and how lovingly they look after each other. Those who are depressed, or whose parents are splitting up, or whose siblings are having problems, are given a lot of support from their friends. One of them who was recently going through a family crisis called ours a Sane House. She should have seen me at her age. Mind you, these terms are all relative. Generally, the sanest house is one that isn't yours.

'It's all thanks to PSHE,' says Lydia.

A contribution schools don't get enough credit for.

And both she and Lawrence have sat up watching over drunk, puking partygoers to prevent them passing out and choking on their own vomit.

Aaaah.

And they've been meticulous about not identifying them, including the boy they once took to A&E on a night bus. Maybe it should be renamed *pier* group: it leads you away from the solid ground of familiar territory and safely back again.

'Of course,' I say, 'your generation does drink quite a lot. We used to drink *way* less than teenagers do now.'

'I can't believe you're saying this,' says Lawrence. 'It's ridiculous.'

'In a typical night at the pub,' I say, 'when I was fifteen, sixteen, we'd have about two halves of lager, max; the boys a bit more. Maybe two or three pints. The most I ever drank in one night was a pint and a half.'

'What? No way!'

'You went to the *pub*??'

'Yeah. Some places just used to chuck us out because we were too young. But at our regular, the owners knew us and kept an eye on us. You didn't misbehave or they'd bar you.'

They are amazed.

'We didn't have the money to drink that much anyhow. And no one drank shorts.'

'Shorts? What are *shorts*?'

'Gin and whatever. Spirits.'

They find this quite astonishing and take every opportunity from now on to bring up my under-age pub-going as proof of my supposedly debauched youth. It does seem ironic that we who were allowed illegally into pubs drank so little, while this generation, who have to show ID for everything, drink so much more. I didn't know anyone who'd had their stomach pumped.

As for drugs, we haven't really discussed them since that homework of Lawrence's in Year Five. As it happens, I've just read a helpful article in the paper which advises:

Resist the temptation to show how 'cool' you are by sharing stories of your own drug taking.

Aha.

I sense an opportunity.

'Kids,' I say, 'have I ever told you about the time I fell down the stairs of a club after three large rum and Cokes and quite a lot of dope?'

I was with a guy who was several years older: at least twenty-six. You bought the Bacardi in half-filled bottles – not half-bottles – then filled them up with the Coke, and everyone was smoking weed. I soon passed the point where even bad dancing was possible, then abruptly realized I had to get outside. But the club was below ground, and the stairs seemed to go up a long way.

'I got about halfway up, then felt myself falling backwards, and my head bounced onto the floor, as if in slow motion. But it didn't hurt. Then I somehow got up, got up the rest of the stairs to the exit, and threw up outside.'

Skunk? This was *Badger*.

'How awful,' shudders Lydia, not – I fear – at the possibility that I might have had a head injury, but the thought of everyone turning to stare.

The bouncer was very kind; he stayed with me, and I did my best to aim away from his shoes.

What I don't tell them is that my so-called boyfriend at the time stayed put because I'd embarrassed him in public, and only took me home in the hope of some post-puke sex. Nor do I add that when we got to my place, the minicab driver joined in trying to persuade me to let that dickhead come upstairs. When I edged myself delicately through my front door and closed it behind me, they were still talking.

So this too – as they say – is a Thing. Not: how to prevent their peer group from convincing them to take drugs – which assumes they have no will of their own – but how to raise kids with enough self-esteem not to end up dating a so-called adult who has no concern for their welfare. My pier group, had they been there, would have done better.

Saw, Starring Lauren Bacall

Lydia's been on about having a fringe.

I've always talked her out of it on the grounds that she shouldn't hide her lovely face. But she's eighteen and a half now, so I no longer have a say.

It's a challenge, getting a teenage girl to even *hear* the words 'lovely face' without emitting an agonized cry and fleeing the room – but she's just about managed to tolerate it, and each time the threat has been seen off.

Today, though, she comes in with the fringe already cut, and it's also rather short.

It's not quite a wacky, *Amelie*-style *'Je suis une* cute kooky French girl' one, thank God, but definitely well shy of her eyebrows. On the plus side, we can see her eyes without having to bend down and peer up at them as if reaching under a sink to examine a U-bend.

'Wow,' I say. 'You look like a 1940s film star.'

'Er, thanks!'

'Where did you go?'

'What d'you mean? Nowhere.'

'For the fringe. You did it yourself?'

A bit defensively:

'Yeah.'

Because they do care what you think.

'Wow. Well done: it looks great.'

She looks genuinely pleased.

Her hair is still slightly reddish from being coloured months ago, and she reminds me a little of Rita Hayworth, my father's favourite star, and then I start thinking about him, and how he never got to meet his granddaughter – or either of them for that matter, and how pleased he would have been.

Sob!

It was not that long ago I packed her off to a friend's 'Hollywood' party in a checked suit I found in a charity shop as Lauren Bacall – specifically, Lauren Bacall in *To Have and Have Not*.

And I don't know how I got away with it, because not only did I make her watch the 'You know how to whistle, don't you, Steve?' scene on YouTube several times – 'The suit's almost an exact match, look!'– I also forced her to go in my actual 1940s shoes – 'Omigod d'you realize they were made the same year as the film?!' – which are really not that comfortable.

Then she waved her own hair, which looked totally authentic, *and* submitted to having her picture taken, leaning forward with one shoulder just like Bacall in the publicity stills for the film.

And now, seeing the fringe, I realize that was probably the last time I will have had an influence on the way she looked. Maybe we should have marked it with some kind of ceremony.

And I suppose, after the numerous Clothes Wars over the years, it seems only fair that she should now ignore my preference, take the initiative and cut herself a fringe.

'Are you going somewhere nice to show it off?'

'Katarina's. I'm going to help her reconfigure some shelves.'

'Here you go.'

Peter comes in with a set of Allen keys, a drill and a saw.

Katarina has moved to a new flat, only a twenty-minute walk away. Peter's desperate for Brexit to be overturned so she'll give up any idea of ever returning to Slovakia.

It's so near Lydia can stroll over there easily, show her the new fringe and imbibe a shot of her sparkling can-do energy while they do the shelves.

But it's on the way to getting dark, and I can feel

my head starting to fill up with all the disasters that could possibly befall a physically fit, capable eighteen-year-old on a twenty minute walk in an area she knows well. As they get older I'm managing to worry a *bit* less; Lawrence is surviving in Manchester, after all, without me sleeping on his floor. But I wonder if that only puts a heavier burden on his sister.

'So . . . just text when you're leaving,' I say casually.

'What do you mean?'

She hasn't left yet, so that would mean texting me from the hall in about five minutes.

'I mean, text me when you leave Katarina's, later. You know. So we know when to expect you.'

'Why? What's the point?'

'So . . . If you don't turn up, we'll go out and look for you.'

'If I get mugged it's not going to make any difference!'

'Well, yeah, but – there are these men in cars . . .'

In my own defence this is true: among the more recent attempted abductions in our area, a man got out of a green Vauxhall and tried to grab a three-year-old off his bike, and a man in a red car followed a fourteen-year-old two streets from here; she hid in one of the front gardens until he'd gone.

'Fourteen,' said one of the neighbours. 'So at least he wasn't a paedophile.'

But even the failed ones can haunt you. Given how rare these incidents are, it seems a bit unfair that we've ended up in some kind of sex offender hotspot.

She puts down her bag and looks at me with her patient face.

'I'm eighteen: I've done this loads of times already, and I'm going to be doing it loads more in the future.'

'I know. You're right. I'm sorry.'

'I'll walk away from the roadside, *OK*? Now can I *go*?'

I consider repeating the advice I first gave her and Lawrence when they were small – to scream, kick, get their DNA etc. – but this time, I manage to hold back.

She picks up her backpack and puts in the bottle of wine from us to Katarina with the drill, the saw and the Allen keys. And the front door swings shut.

'Isn't it great to see her going off, with her saw and her Allen keys?' says Peter.

He sees my expression.

'What? You OK?'

'Mm. Yeah.'

I don't want him to know I'm worrying instead of applauding her confidence. He's right: it *is* great. And

I try to remember there hasn't been an incident for a few years now. Also, I realize how much she's *his* daughter as well as mine: self-possessed, fast on her feet, and now really quite handy with a saw.

Exit Group

I'm going to meet Peter at our friends Tim and Sheila's for dinner, about forty minutes across town.

Peter's coming from somewhere else, and I set off in the car in plenty of time. I know most of the route by heart and will just use the phone for the last bit. I get most of the way with no problems, and once I'm quite near I stop and get out the phone. But the map won't load.

So I pull over beside a man in a parked car and gesture politely to get his attention. Then I add an extra friendly smile. But he won't respond or roll down the window, just starts trying to pull out round me to drive away – which he can't. I continue gesturing; how many reasons could a fairly sane-looking female in a car have for stopping beside a man? Does he think I'm soliciting? Unusual, if good for tax deductible mileage and extra seat covers. A mugger? I'd have to get out and walk round to get anywhere near his wallet. Eventually, realizing he can't pull out until I've gone, he reluctantly puts down the window and pretends to be amazed when I ask for directions.

'Oh! Yes, it's right then left, then right: off the main road, which is just up there.'

I want to say: *Well, what did you think I wanted?* But I thank him and continue on my way. Then I realize I don't know which end of the main road I need, and it's a T-junction. Again, the map won't load. So I flag down a young woman with a phone.

'Have you got satnav?' she asks.

'Yes, but it won't load.'

'Bless!'

She actually says this.

So, in the space of ten minutes I've been perceived as both threatening *and* past it. Surely they should cancel each other out?

And I hate the fact that if the device fails, it's the human that's at fault.

The next day Lawrence is home again, gazing into a bowl of last night's mashed potato like a medium whose ectoplasm has unexpectedly hardened before take-off.

'I might do hash browns,' he says thoughtfully.

'With the mash? Isn't that meant to be with chopped or diced?'

'No it isn't. It's meant to be with mash.'

The 'you are mad' look flickers across his face.

It's 10.30 and he hasn't had breakfast yet, which is the equivalent of about two days without eating for a normal person. For us, one hour is like six. If either of us has low blood sugar, a row can erupt from nought to meltdown in five seconds. If *neither* of us has eaten, Peter and Lydia tend to grab their magazines and flee upstairs, like the drinkers in a Western saloon when the bad guys ride in. Luckily I've had a boiled egg.

'Well, when I first had them, in New York – where I think they probably *invented* them – the potato was diced. With onion. It was delicious actually—'

'And how many centuries ago was that?'

'Er . . .'

A smile threatens to break out so I look down.

'And had the potato masher been invented? Or did they have to tread the potatoes?'

He demonstrates, stepping up and down exaggeratedly behind the counter. Lydia looks up from the sketches for her bed design, and says:

'They used to do the laundry at the same time: just rinse off the potatoes.'

'Ha!'

In a sequence that is now familiar and predictable, this has ceased being about how you make hash browns and become their rolling version of the Monty Python

'Four Yorkshiremen' sketch, their supposedly hilarious fantasy idea of my past, where children Went Up the Chimney and Down the Mine and there was no pop music or television, only huge wirelesses driven by steam. Admittedly, I probably brought this on myself by telling them that when we were quite small, my sister and I once asked our dad: 'What was it like when you were alive?'

Lawrence looks up hash browns on his phone.

'You can use mashed, diced, chopped, riced –'

'Like the Swiss dish rosti,' I say.

'Yes, like the Swiss dish rosti – or "any type of *cooked potato*".'

He emphasizes 'cooked potato' as if he is Walter Raleigh explaining the exotic root vegetable to the Tudors for the first time.

'Exactly,' I say. 'Just as I said.'

He looks at me, rolls his eyes again and says,

'I think I'll have avocado on toast.'

'Sorry, no bread.'

'Then I'll just have to spread it on my hand.'

'Like we used to do, in the time before bread. Or,' I say, 'I could make you some poached eggs.'

This is one of the few things left that I make better than him, or it was – until I rashly told him the magic ingredient is vinegar.

'So you don't really need me to make them any more.'

'I knew that already, though.'

'Oh. Then my time on earth is done.'

'But that sounds really good. Yeah, poached eggs on . . .'

'A – plate.'

He smiles.

I put on the kettle.

'It really does seem to be costing us far too much.'

He gives me the 'you are mad' look again.

'To boil the kettle.'

At the weekend I cut out a table of energy usage from the paper and stuck it on the cupboard door above the tea and coffee area, where it raises my anxiety levels to no good purpose.

In order to reduce our electricity costs I've been trying to interest Peter in a kettle you boil once in the morning that stays hot for four hours, but, as people once did with the telephone, he wants to wait a while – say ten years, and see if it catches on. By which time the microchips in our brains will probably be able to give us the refreshing sensation of having had a cup of tea, with no boiling or drinking required, just like *Total Recall* – or perhaps *Total Reboil*.

'It'd pay for itself in a month,' I say. 'I mean, look

at how often we boil the bloody thing – at least six times a day, and with you lot here—'

'Sorry,' says Lawrence.

'No, you know I don't mean that – I'm just saying it's often, that's all. And when friends come round . . .'

Lawrence opens his mouth.

'And don't apologize for having friends.'

As is the typical reaction around here when I complain about something, no one appears to take any notice, but for the rest of the day, Lawrence responds in his customary 'amusing' way.

'Do you want pasta for lunch, with home-made pesto? Oh no, wait: it involves boiling the kettle.'

Then he stands beside it, with a kind of helpless, winsome expression presumably meant to be charmingly satirical.

'Just put it on,' I say.

'If you're *sure* . . .'

Just before supper time, he looks closely at the energy usage table and says:

'I know you're really concerned about saving money at the moment, but it really doesn't seem that much.'

'What? £1.39?!'

'Er no: 1.39p. Quite cheap, I'd say.'

'What?'

I can't see Peter, but I feel him smirking behind me.

'It's just that £1.39 isn't generally written as 1.39p. So . . . I think to boil the kettle actually costs less than one and a half pence. Which, you know, doesn't seem that bad.'

A pause.

Of the two parents in this house, I'm the numerate one. I've arranged all our mortgages. I sold Peter's family home after his stepmother died, and sold my father's house and business, then my mother's. I've completed four entire probate applications, for God's sake!

'Well,' I say cheerily. 'You're the one doing the Maths degree, so I suppose you must be right.'

He raises an eyebrow.

But I don't feel cheery at all. I feel like Margaret Thatcher in *The Iron Lady* when she's no longer prime minister and has to learn how to go to a shop and buy milk.

I'm quite disturbed by this. But if I freak out about it, as the children still like to say, it will be much, much worse. The one thing more awful than declining in front of your children is being distressed by it. The only way is to brush it off – make sure they understand it's only happened because you're distracted by more important matters.

'I've been a bit distracted,' I say, 'since Mum died.'

And he puts a comforting arm round me.

'I know.'

Phew. I lean my face against his chest. Then he adds,

'You just sit down over there, and I'll get on with making dinner. You don't want to overstrain yourself now, do you?'

What a relief: he isn't worried or he wouldn't be taking the piss.

I make myself a drink and settle down to check my messages, but my phone is dead and I can't find the charger.

'My charger is missing,' I tell Lawrence. 'Anyone seen it?'

He looks mildly incredulous.

'Er, believe me: no one wants to steal your charger.'

He was fine about the kettle; why is he reacting to a simple enquiry as though I'm accusing my carers of stealing my clothes?

'It's a perfectly reasonable question,' I say. 'People take other people's chargers all the time.'

'Er, they really don't.'

That's it: he really is making me sound paranoid now. But I know if I say that, it will only make it worse. So I stamp upstairs and find it plugged into a socket on the landing, definitely not by me; I know, because I never leave it at floor level, where I have to bend down to get it.

On the phone is a message from the WhatsApp group I recently started for a bunch of us freelancers who meet for coffee every month or so in our local cafe. I couldn't believe how easy it was. Wayhey! I am now – to use an old-fashioned term – bang up to date. I reply 'Yes' to our next meet, and at the end, click on Exit Group.

Ah. Possibly that was the wrong thing. I just meant to close it. I try to go back in to rectify it.

It says: *You are no longer a participant in this group.*

I text my sister, who is even more useless than me, but whose thirteen-year-old son Leo is good at solving problems like this. However, he is at school, selfishly paying attention to his lessons.

I text our friend Patrick.

Rather embarrassing. Have accidentally locked myself out of our Cafe Group. Can you readmit me?

Can't seem to do it. Sorry.

The children appear.

'How do I put myself back into a WhatsApp group?' I ask them.

'No idea,' says Lawrence. 'Google it.'

'Is that your answer to everything?'

'Pretty much.'

'For God's sake . . . Lydia?'

'Yeah. Google it.'

They're the first generation not to have a shared skills pool. If they don't need it, they don't learn it. They don't use WhatsApp, so I may as well ask them how to build a dry-stone wall. It's ridiculous. I don't take milk but I still know how to pour it for other people.

To be fair, we're only able to watch Netflix because Lydia's still mediating the precarious relationship between the TV and the iPad, at least until she moves out. The ultra-temperamental HDMI cable that holds them together flickers off if we do so much as press pause, and only she has the magic touch. And the remote – Stone Age technology which has worked fine for about twelve years – is for some reason suddenly only effective when pointed at a certain angle at the bottom left-hand corner of the TV – *by her*. It's like Richard Pryor's description of the way to the female orgasm – so nuanced as to be beyond man, literally.

'Why does nothing in this house work properly?' says Lawrence as he drifts unhelpfully past; almost the exact same thing I used to say to my mother, except at her place it was true.

'Of course, you know you bought the wrong telly,' adds Lydia, as she goes off to repaint another doll.

Where are the superfast techie teenagers we were promised? These only go at half the speed, and often provide no service at all.

While I wait for Netflix to get in the mood I Google 'How to rejoin a WhatsApp group'. It says: *Contact the Group Admin.*

I feel like the ill-fated hero of a novel I read once, who, during a particularly cold winter, accidentally locks himself out of the house and tries to get back in via the cat flap – as you do – and gets his head stuck but can't reverse out again either, and freezes to death on his own porch.

The next day I'm in our local M&S, passing my 'belly button' pasta across the scanner, and the Voice says:

'Have you scanned your Sparks card?'

And I think:

'FFS! Can't you wait until I've finished? That is *So Annoying.*'

I can't stand self-checkouts; they cut jobs and there's nowhere to put anything down. And I'm irritated by the Sparks card and its ridiculously narrow special offers, like: '20% off pineapple desserts and size 16 nude shapewear' – which you also have to go online and click on. Could they make it any more of a pain? I always bring it, though.

The Voice sounds all smooth and reasonable, but is actually really micro-managey and controlling.

Then I realize what it reminds me of. Or rather, *who*.

What did Lawrence say, shortly before he moved out?

'Can you not interrupt me to tell me to do *another* thing before I've even begun doing the *first* thing you wanted me to do?'

That's what happens when you let checkouts be voiced by mothers. There should be a Teenage Response Button you can press that snaps back:

'NO: I WILL IN A MINUTE! JUST STOP GOING *ON* AT ME, WILL YOU?!'

This is something they don't tell you when you're thinking of becoming an Older Mother: your kids' rapidly increasing competence at this stage, when they're roaring out of the pits firing on all cylinders, coincides exactly with your progression towards decrepitude. And it's dawning on me, with a dreadful, sinking sensation, that it's only going to get worse.

It's a strong argument in favour of becoming a Teenage Parent. When they're fifteen you'll only be, say, thirty-two: in full possession of your faculties, instead of fifty- or sixty-something and increasingly defeated by the modern world. I didn't go to university and no one's ever asked to see my two useless A levels. So just think – instead of going to the pub and not reading *The Winter's Tale* I could have been having these two and be one step ahead of them all the time, instead of the pathetic object of their disdain.

Except they wouldn't *be* these two, so I suppose I've got the better deal after all.

Ages 18 to 20:
Toys R No Longer Us

Lydia is off to another festival and has left a huge black sack of God knows what in the hall.

'Lyd! Can you please put away this bag of – whatever it is?'

'It's the last of my cuddly toys. You're always telling me to get rid of them. Well, now I am.'

Actually, I am *not* always telling her to get rid of them. I am always telling her to *tidy them up*, which is not the same thing.

'Hang on – can I look through them?'

'Why?'

'No reason.'

Our friend Sarah B has recently suffered a shock: after months of begging followed by a stand-off, her daughter abruptly tidied her room before moving out.

And others we know have been caught off guard by this unexpected personality change. The young person is off to be furtherly educated in some distant town, abandoning a festering chamber of one-legged Darth Vaders, mangy stuffed animals and vintage tat. So the hapless parent nags them to tidy their bloody room or they won't be going anywhere.

Then suddenly – in these rare but not unique cases – they *do*.

And the poor parent panics as they see – in Sarah's words – 'practically their whole childhood' being flung into the rubbish. Karen, who has three boys, gets up and mimes trying to catch a spray of tiny little shorts before they hit the black sack, while Sarah does a touching imitation of herself holding up a manky top redolent of infant memories and making a tragic mewing sound.

Also, there may be something buried in there that Lydia's made herself, and I'm discreetly saving her early pieces for when she's successful and we can flog them off to pay the carers.

I open the bag and take out:

• A Hallmark teddy holding a tiny star-shaped cushion with a gold 'L' on it.
• A 'lifesize' mauve unicorn hobby horse with only the head left – the stick having been used for something else, possibly poking her brother – looking as if recently shot and ready for mounting on a shield.

- A soft brown horse in reclining pose, like Manet's Olympia: 'The first I bought with my own money.'
- A small fluffy puppy brought back by me from Dublin, formerly in green bag with shamrock.
- Official Peter Rabbit 'merch', misshapen from excessive cuddling and being repeatedly thrown.
- Kangaroo with label saying 'My name is Matilda' brought from Australia by Peter's friend Jason, with tiny fluffy Joey in pouch and jagged tear in tummy resembling emergency Caesarean scar where Joey was abruptly removed for deployment in another game.
- Faintly smirking knitted duck in mauve bonnet, suggestive of one of those 'alternative' adaptations of Jane Austen.
- Naturalistic soft small tiger (standing).
- Little furry hedgehog with what looks like a plastic picture of a lobster round its neck.

I ask: 'Why has it got a picture of a lobster round its neck?'

'It's a *starsign hedgehog*. Scorpio? I got it at the airport in Italy.'

- Dalmatian sewn into its kennel – with no visible back legs – as if it's been through the matter transporting machine in *The Fly*.

- Baby fox: her first Sew it Yourself kit.
- Hand-knitted rabbit finger puppet with a vaguely melancholy expression.
- Puppy finger puppet from Jellycat.
- Arctic fox brought from America by another of Peter's friends.
- Two little dolls with wool hair, one in yellow gingham, one in green, both in slightly smeared lipstick like the aftermath of a school trip that's ended in a mass shoplifting spree at Superdrug.
- Tiger key ring from London Zoo.
- Soft frog key ring.
- Soft camel key ring.
- Pink satin frog with bronze appliqué shapes on its back that are presumably meant to be frog-like, but more closely resemble the medieval skin disease in *Game of Thrones*.
- Pink, fluffy sphere with dreamy blue face. May have been taking MDMA.
- Soft teddy key ring in blue T-shirt that says 'Friends Always' and a bleary expression, evoking the morning after a hen night.
- Soft pony key ring with too-tight string round neck, suggesting auto-erotic asphyxiation gone awry due to lack of opposable thumbs.
- Blue teddy key ring bought at school fundraiser, or

maybe puppy. Possibly both gender and species fluid.

- About twenty-five items of Build a Bear clothing, including Dalmatian-pattern playsuit with inset sleeves, Velcro closure and tail, made by Lydia.

And this is just the final bag.

'I just want to say, Lydia: well done for having that clear-out.'

'Yeah, because I need the space for something else. Well, sort of . . .'

Can you guess what our eighteen-year-old daughter wants next in her life?

'They've got some at the Emmaus Shop.'

A worthy venture, where knackered household appliances are reconditioned and sold on by the long-term unemployed, and the funds used for training them in useful skills.

She wants a freezer.

Immediately I envisage her opening the lid and loading in a whole deer, probably because I like venison and we haven't had supper yet.

'Just a small one. So I can keep my dead animals in it – for stuffing. And I don't have to take up so much space in the family one.'

There's currently a blue tit in there next to the ice cream, and another squirrel, plus there's a fox pelt in a box beside the back door. Oh, and the wood-pecker.

The landline had rung – a rare event in itself. Lawrence picked up.

'Lydia, phone! A woodpecker for you: it's coming round after lunch.'

I knew word had spread, but surely not to the extent that the local wildlife had begun turning itself in.

'It was Mrs H from school,' said Lydia. 'She found it on the balcony outside the dining block. It must have flown into a window.'

The only creature more desperate to get in than the parents.

So we haven't yet had to evict the prawns and chicken thighs. But I don't want to make it too easy, especially as one of her friends rang last week to say she'd seen a dead fox in the road, and Lydia persuaded Peter to take her in the car to get it. He admitted he wasn't fully behind the idea.

'But I didn't want to be a killjoy, you know. I didn't want to be the Person Who Says No.'

'God forbid: that's my role.'

'But there were quite a few flies round it. Then to my relief a Highway Maintenance van pulled up and we hid behind a tree.'

'So where's this freezer going to go then . . .?'

'Um . . .'

I say it can go in the shed. She gets a modestly sized one for £25 from her savings, and we also pick up some £1 DVDs.

'You'll have to rearrange things and tidy up to make space.'

'Of course! Thank you! You won't regret this, I promise.'

For some reason the phrase 'you won't regret this' fills me with apprehension.

That autumn, Peter goes to Australia to see his old friend Jason, and brings her back a kangaroo skull – what else? – Jason found on his own land.

'I suppose you didn't find any whole pelts to stuff?'

'Sorry, darling.'

'This is great though!'

There's just one teensy problem.

There's something moving about inside.

Lydia puts it in a spare test tube she happens to have, and Peter calls his friend James, who has the most eclectic contacts list probably in the country.

'I brought this kangaroo skull back from Melbourne, and there seems to be a very small live spider in it. Obviously, being Australian, it could be poisonous.'

Not to mention probably illegal. Of all the challenges

I anticipated with teenagers, I can honestly say that the accidental importation of potentially lethal non-native arthropods in the partial skeletons of marsupials was not on the list.

'Don't worry,' he says. 'I probably know someone who can deal with this. I'll pop round and get it.'

He puts it in a little box with some water, then emails a photograph to London Zoo, two pet shops and Heathrow Animal Reception, where thousands of impounded creatures live out their days in a kind of eternal transfer lounge. They'll take it, but Heathrow's a bit far, so he calls a pet shop in Wales, which puts him onto a man in Sutton, which is a lot nearer: a collector who has 170 in his otherwise normal terraced house. He takes the box, identifies it as a white-tailed spider – *Lampona cylindrata*, not fatal to humans – and gives James a medal: 'For Services to Arachnology'.

'Well done, spider,' says Lydia, 'surviving all that way. And James too.'

Thank God it was too small to stuff.

The woodpecker that came from school to us seemed an appropriate beginning of the end, as Churchill might have said, of Lydia's fourteen years of formal education. For we have reached her last day of school, ever.

At 2 p.m. she will become a Neet – Not in Education, Employment or Training – and Peter and I will finally be Neeps: Not in Education, Employment or Parenting.

I watch her getting ready for the programme of *Total Wipeout*-style activities that's been organized on the playing fields for the last day.

'I'm so glad you didn't listen to me,' I say. 'About the fringe.'

'It's part of growing up though, isn't it?' she says. 'Stopping listening to your parents.'

'I suppose you're right.'

'And going out and getting drunk all the time . . .'

I glance across at her.

'JOKING.'

'Yeah . . . But – don't make that a template for the rest of your life.'

She looks at me and grins.

'TOO LATE!'

And she's gone.

Proceed to Checkout

The main difference between Lawrence's sixteenth birthday and this, his twentieth, is that now he can cook. But to save him the hassle, I offer to order party food from M&S.

We sit and deliberate together over each item in the copious selection. One of the surprising and rather welcome side effects of his becoming a student is that he is reluctant to spend very much, even of our money.

'Go on,' I say. 'Have *two* trays of wontons: it is your twentieth.'

Eventually, with a bit of persuasion, he chooses enough mini thingies for everyone to have at least three each, and we go to buy the drinks.

It's only the day before the event that I realize I've had no confirmation email.

I have failed to check out! And the do is less than thirty-six hours away so we can't order the wontons and party-size samosas and little prawn twiddly things.

'I am so so *sorry*.'

'Actually,' he says, 'that's good in a way – because now I can do a barbecue.'

It is August after all, and we have a garden.

So we go and get a great pile of chicken breasts, which he marinates in oil and beer and various other things from Marlena Spieler's *Classic Barbecue and Grill Cook Book*, and several packs of wraps. Then he makes fresh guacamole and tzatziki, and when his friends arrive, they can customize their own wraps.

Peter and I mind the barbecue, replenish the salad elements, eat the burned and too-small pieces of chicken and chat to his friends, in our new role as powerless constitutional monarchs brought out for festivals and public holidays.

The ones we've known since primary school bring us up to date with their lives, and I compliment the one who's got something on SoundCloud – with a kind of filial satnav burbling in my ear: *beware of uncool adjectives, stick to neutral terms like 'great', don't compare it with some obscure track from the 1970s that no one's heard of – and do NOT under any circumstances tell him you've been dancing round the kitchen to it.*

I hope Lawrence notices how well I'm doing with the self-censorship. Succeeding in not copying my mother – 'As it happens I *do* know how to keep secrets: for instance . . .' – means he can't praise me for what I haven't said. But I will award myself a Non-Embarrassing half-blue.

At about ten, they all get ready to leave for a club. As part of his present we're going to clear up.

As they all head in from the garden towards the front door, forming a loose line through the kitchen, they look a bit as though they're off on a school outing, albeit one with roll-ups and bottles of beer. I slightly want to ask if they've all remembered their £1.50 to get a pencil in the museum shop.

Several say thank you for the party, and some even give us a hug.

'We must treasure this moment,' says Peter.

'I'm treasuring,' I say, as we scrape the dirty plates.

And afterwards it seems like a vignette of a death; the washing and mopping and roll-ups in the plant pots fade away and the beautiful, animated young faces remain.

Photo Finish

When they were babies, I began two photo albums. During the weekends and, later on, the school holidays, I'd take them out, have a look at the loose photos I'd thrown in, and resolve to start putting them in properly when I had time. The aim was to give them one each, to take with them when they moved out.

'Because,' as Lawrence said, 'when we're packing to go off to university, a massively huge *photo album* will be top of the list.'

Still I carried on, musing, choosing, swapping, and drifting off into reveries. It's the ideal displacement activity and a harmless conduit for nostalgia.

I stop and look at one particular picture, of them laughing together on a beach. It was taken when they were only eleven and ten. But something about the pose, with Lawrence leaning up on one elbow, makes them appear older. It's as if you can glimpse the teenagers within.

Lydia comes in and points out a picture of us on holiday in the Canary Islands.

'You look really good there.'

'Are you sure? I don't think so at all.'

All I can see are my fat knees, that were once quite shapely. The day we got married I had great knees. The angle of the shot is unfortunate; I think Peter must have been crouching, so the shot looked up at my thighs, exacerbated by my too-short holiday skirt. On the plus side, taking photographs is the closest he ever gets to adoring me on bended knee.

And now she looks quite annoyed.

'Yes! You look great! What's wrong with you?'

And I realize, with a great fat whammy to the brain, that I have no more idea whether I look good or not than any other woman. Quite often, in fact, I only see the flaws. Me! Who's always telling others to be more confident.

What makes this really unsettling is that when I look at myself in the mirror I'm not *repulsed*. I don't think I'm ugly, wizened or fat. I think I look all right for someone who eats a bit more than necessary and could take more exercise. But when I *speak*, none of that comes out.

'Of course!' you say. 'You don't want to be *boasting*. You don't want to go around like that woman in the

Daily Mail who thought women resented her for being too good looking' – and who they *did* resent, but for being a big-headed show-off.

No. But I have a daughter. And it should be the law that all women with girls in their care are forcibly prevented from self-criticism – of any physical aspect of themselves whatsoever, unless it's 'Got a bit sunburned there,' or, 'Stubbed my toe tripping over the doorway of that pub.'

Yet somehow, I – who eat what I like, don't go on diets, never apologize for the state of my bottom, or any other part of me, and have raised a daughter who eats normally – turn out to have the same affliction as millions of others: I look at myself through shit-tinted glasses.

And she has brought me to this realization.

I thought I was immune. I honestly, sincerely believed I didn't have the Problem.

'Me? I'm wonderfully rational and balanced: I don't hate my body at all.'

And I don't. It's just that I have some sort of troll inside, rewriting my lines.

Which is such a pity, because all these years I've been telling Lydia how lovely she is, my Inner Female has been pulling in the opposite direction.

Lydia says:

'You are quite negative sometimes, you know.'

And the best I can do – in fact all I can do – is not deny it.

Planned Obsolescence

Lydia burns her hand draining a pan of pasta. So I say:

'Put it under the cold tap.'

And she says:

'I *know*. You don't have to tell me: I know what to do!'

'I know you know,' I say. 'It's just a reflex. I'd say the same to Peter. It's what you say when you care. It's not a literal explanation of what to do.'

'Well, whatever. I don't need you to *tell* me.'

'I'm just – connecting,' I say, feebly.

'Just leave me alone, OK?'

'OK. So do you still want me to take you to Sainsbury's, or what?'

She's having some friends over for her nineteenth birthday, and we've arranged for us – Peter and me – to help with the food, then go over to Sarah B's for supper.

This will work well. We can serve the food, say

hello to her friends, then go to Sarah's, where despite work and the number of children – four, with three still at home – there is always a proper meal to be had. Peter says the more children people have the more relaxed they become, which I'm sure is true, but I'd rather not pay such a high price to prove it.

At Sainsbury's we pause for a short discussion before selecting each item. My idea to get My Little Pony napkins isn't well received, even though I suggest buying them ironically.

When we get back I make a double lot of pizza dough, using the recipe from the back of the yeast packet, which works even when you're two gins in, and set about arranging the room for her guests.

Lydia and I are preparing her party together – this is so nice!

'And are you sure you don't want me to do a cake?'

'Viola's doing one. Sorry.'

'Great. I'm not looking for more things to do. Where would you like the glasses?'

'It's OK – we can manage.'

What?

I've barely got started.

She can't even cook!

But the Boyfriend can. And he's on his way.

'So you don't want me to do the mini pizzas?'

'No.'

'The ones I made last year.'

'No.'

'That your friends said they really liked.'

She looks at me. I feel like the last miner at the pit, trying to stop them closing the gates.

'And I liked them too, just . . .'

'OK! So, what about moving the table and all the chairs and – whatever.'

'Viola's coming to help with that.'

Whoa! Can we just slow down a minute here?

When Lawrence has his friends round he always lets us stay for a bit, at least till our bedtime. We were even invited to his New Year's Eve drinks, as long as we didn't tidy up while they were still there.

Should I quote this?

'Your brother can vouch for us. Here's a reference . . .'

The Boyfriend arrives. He's made pizza for us before; he arranged the slices of mushroom, red pepper, etc. in neat concentric patterns all calmly, without Making a Thing of It.

Is he going to use my dough?

'Hi,' I say. 'I made some dough for you. It's in there, keeping warm.'

'Great,' he says. 'Thanks.'

'OK,' says Lydia. 'We can take it from here.'

'What, you're going to do all of it?'

'Yeah. Just, you know, piss off. In a good way.'

I'm reminded of a not entirely pleasant sensation from my distant past. Ah yes: being outside the red rope in front of a club, and watching the cool people sweep past.

'OK,' I say. 'I'll just check you've got enough mozzarella . . .'

'We just bought it, so obviously we've got enough.'

'And – I'll just put away all these bags; you don't want it looking like the Mind shop.'

She glares at me: charity shops are to her as wayside shrines to Buddhists. And Mind is a favourite.

'Thanks. You can go.'

'Right. Have a lovely time. We will have to come back, though, later. But we won't interrupt – we'll just go quietly upstairs, and—'

'*Duh*. Just – *go*. OK?'

As ever when I need backup, Peter has vanished. I go upstairs to find him on the bed, reading a biography of Enzo Ferrari.

'OMG, that's it,' I say. 'She's down there, doing it all – with Him and Viola the Wonder Friend: all the food and *everything*. We're redundant.'

'You may be,' he says.

'Oh, ha ha.'

But it's true.

In the future, our children will call on him to fix their babies' cots – if we're still alive by then – and to adjust their stairgates so they can open and close them without taking a finger off. He'll be building Wendy houses and making flyovers out of Meccano for the Brio train set we're keeping. And when the whole social order goes tits up because we've run out of coal and oil and can't make enough electricity because *that* needs coal as well, he'll be one of the lynchpins of the new order along with the blacksmiths and game poachers, while the useless, artistic Calmans will be the first to be hunted down and eaten.

Actually, he has already begun to upload parts of his brain to Lydia. She's learning painting and decorating, how to use a Rawlplug, how to make a template to fit sheet flooring, how to use plywood offcuts to box off an exposed gas pipe and how to get half a plastic plug pin out of a socket where it's snapped off, using a drill bit not much thicker than a pin. Actually, that last one she came up with herself. So it's clear that with her knitting and sewing as well, she'll always be able to support herself and probably a family too. Not that I'm saying she should have children, obviously.

So we can die pretty much anytime from now on,

and she'll be fine. Come to think of it, she's *so* handy maybe we can avoid the whole Student Loan Interest Extortion Experience and send her to straight out to work. Of all my mother's friends – and they were an intellectual bunch – the handiest was the one the Nazis stopped from going to university, whose parents got her apprenticed to a joiner. Contrary to popular belief, Jews can do DIY; it just takes extreme circumstances to make them.

As for me, all I know how to do is make orange cake with ground almonds and never to take out an interest-only mortgage if you can avoid it. And since he's doing a Maths degree, and has already far outpaced me in the kitchen, Lawrence has those covered.

It's strange to think that Lydia resembles my mother, but also Peter's father – whom she never met. He and Peter's mother married during rationing, and he made all their furniture: bookcases, bureau, drop-leaf dining table, wardrobe and chairs. He could also pull over into a layby and make tea on one of those little wobbly gas burners without setting fire to his sleeves. My father, by contrast, was not at all handy round the house, and even less so out of it. Where Lydia has already made an actual bed, he couldn't even tuck in a sheet properly. Or wouldn't. And I take after him – i.e. the wrong parent.

It was my mother who would have been indispensable after the apocalypse. With her recall of pretty much every bird, berry and root, she would have been able to help the survivors – survive.

'That's potato and *that's* deadly nightshade,' I can hear her saying. 'Same family, but don't put the wrong one in your shepherd's pie.'

It's the botanical equivalent of knowing which wire to cut when defusing a bomb. She could also distinguish a harmless, non-stinging hoverfly from a wasp. Unfortunately, whenever she tried to pass on any of this invaluable knowledge, I was never paying attention.

The only skills I *can* deploy from her repertoire are how to put your hair up so it doesn't fall down, how to make a crêpe paper flower, and how to make a little house out of a cardboard box. None of which will be much use post-apocalyptically – except possibly the last one.

On our way out to Sarah's I answer the door to two boys I've never seen before.

Smile. Be welcoming. Do not turn into your father.

My friends were quite nervous around him, and he was even fiercer with males. However, when I ask them who they are, the flicker of nervousness that passes across their faces is quite satisfying.

When we come back the party's in full swing and we tiptoe upstairs.

At 1.45 a.m. I wake up. The kitchen door is wide open, allowing us full benefit of the music and quite a bit of shrieking. I get up and go and ask them to keep it down a bit, again trying not to transform, Hulk style, into my dad and ensuring Lydia never invites me to any future birthday of hers, ever.

In the morning we get up extra late to leave them time to clear up, and find a note propped against the kettle:

> *We are very sorry about the noise last night. We have cleared up (washing up, mopping floor, dustpan crumbs etc.). Let me know if I missed anything. Help yourselves to some of Viola's delicious cake.*
>
> *Love from*
> *Lydia + Friends XOXOXO*

'My God,' says Peter. 'What did you say to them?'

'Great. They clear up and I get the blame. You're welcome.'

How am I going to stand it here, just with him?

A Sense of Direction

Lydia's applying to art school and needs a portfolio to carry her pictures, which are currently spread all over the dining table and surrounding floor like a gallery after a tornado.

It's exciting: something is happening on the Further Education Front! With lots and lots of paper! And taxidermy and hand-made bras! But it's slightly tricky getting round the room.

'We love having them here,' I say. 'It's just . . .'

'Don't worry, it will all be cleared away soon,' she says.

'No, no: we don't want them to be gone. We just want to be able to get to the washing machine, and – maybe have people round to dinner again one day. *Joking*!'

Neither of us is feeling at all jokey at the moment. She feels under huge pressure to get in, and I feel under huge pressure to keep encouraging her to fill the portfolio, while not micro-managing. Because while in a marriage asking equals nagging, in a parent–child relationship *encouraging* is nagging, and helping is *micro-managing*.

And saying:

'If you don't get *on* with it instead of watching another fifteen bloody episodes of *Friends* you'll never get in, will you?' is counterproductive.

Who knew?

She doesn't have a portfolio large enough. So we have to get one. And this is good, because we can carry out a really simple task and come back with a sense of achievement.

'You don't have to come with me, but I'd quite like the company,' she says.

'Of course, I'd love to.'

I'm needed!

You can get portfolios in A4, A3, A2 and A1 – which is almost the size of my desk. She needs A1.

'Do we really need this size?' I say.

'You don't: I do.'

She's right. She's got enough work here to fill a wardrobe.

Luckily, there's a superb art supplies shop only a short bus ride away.

'It's opposite the hospital,' I say.

'That doesn't mean anything to me,' she says.

'Of course it does. It's a huge, well-known local landmark. It's been on *24 Hours in A&E*.'

I have an innately Good Sense of Direction and Excellent Spatial Memory, so when I say the art shop is opposite the hospital, I know I'm right.

She looks down at her phone.

'It's opposite Nando's.'

Injury, deterioration and death versus peri-peri chicken: the disparate priorities of the generations.

'It's opposite the hospital,' I say. 'Plus it's the name of the bus stop that they announce in the annoyingly cheery voice.'

The Voice – who sounds as though she's been directed to give 'More, darling! *More!*' – is at best irritating, and, in the area we're going to, grotesquely incongruous.

'The next stop is Grimy Towers!' she gushes, like Mary Poppins on ecstasy, as you pass the enormous psychiatric hospital and the block of flats where three women and three children died eight years before Grenfell in a similarly preventable fire. But High Mary Poppins sails past as if she's just seen that rainbow merry-go-round, but loaded with naked men holding cream cakes. Maybe going through really rich areas they should do the opposite, and get Ken Loach:

'Park Lane: alight here for unearned wealth and privilege, and property owned by non-tax-paying offshore corporations and violently repressive Wahhabist monarchies.'

'The map says it's opposite Nando's,' she says again. 'And I believe the map. OK?'

So why don't I just shut up and get on the bloody bus?

Is it because in the modern world, with a nineteen- and a twenty-year-old, I feel increasingly less relevant and useful, and ever more eager to deploy the few traditional skills I still have, like my Sense of Direction? I fear it is.

'See?' I say, when Ecstatic Mary Poppins announces the stop. We get off and cross over, and discover the shop is not quite where I thought.

'It's a bit hard to find,' I say, as we get nearer to the next bus stop, the one for Nando's. 'Being hidden behind the main road.'

It's a pleasing quirk of London that moments from Grimy Towers there exists a haven bursting with every size and colour of paper, infinite colours of paint, easels, stickers, drawing books and paper unicorns to fold.

Once you find it.

So we peer round the back of the next three blocks, but no art shop.

As it's raining, Lydia has put her phone away, with its omniscient map. I have maps on mine too, of course, but I don't need it because I Know Where Everything Is.

Each step we take away from the hospital makes me feel more of an idiot. Pathetically, I try to distract her with trivial observations like: 'Oh look, there's that really cool-looking charity shop that's always closed!'

On we tread, in the rain, till we're almost *two* whole stops away from where we got off, all the way from Grimy Towers to Crazy Junction, with its many criss-crossing lanes.

To my amazement, Lydia does not say: *I told you so, you pig-headed, incredibly annoying woman!* But though I have been let off the recriminations it's noon and I can feel my blood sugar falling: a dangerous portent.

'Why don't I nip into Morrisons,' I say, 'and get a snack, and you can browse?'

But that will defeat the point of going together. On the other hand, I am crashing and need to eat something really *soon*, before I turn into my father and end up screaming at the sales assistant for not providing a wide enough selection of A5 magenta envelopes.

Inevitably we start arguing, even though there are only two A1 folios to choose from, and she examines them both and says she prefers the cheaper one, even though it has a small scuff mark on the front.

'Maybe we should both go to Morrisons now, and get something to eat, so we don't have to drag the folio with us?' she says.

An inspired idea.

So we go into Morrisons, where she finds two large Pizza Express pizzas for £8 and I get a box of their deliciously crisp breadsticks to hold myself together until we get back, plus a jar of Bonne Maman jam as it's on special offer, a bag of sugar as we've run out and a tray of pink primulas for £2. Lydia observes this entirely superfluous – but such good value – acquisition without a murmur.

Then we go back and buy the enormous portfolio, and get a discount for the tiny scuff mark, and manoeuvre it onto the bus, which is crammed with about thirty quite noisy seven-year-olds on a school outing. We roll our eyes at each other and smile; as a common adversary even mildly raucous children are quite bonding.

When we get in we put one of the pizzas in the oven and watch three episodes of *The End of the F-ing World*, a bleakly funny Channel 4 show about two teenagers, a nihilistic girl and a wannabe psychopath, who go on the run after stealing his dad's car and robbing a man who molests the boy in a gents' lavatory.

'I've always wanted to punch my dad in the face,' says the boy in a voiceover; his dad is a complete arse.

And we both shout:

'Well, do it then!'

(He does.)

Later on, after supper, I say:

'I'm really sorry I said the art shop was opposite the hospital. You were right: it *is* opposite Nando's. I feel awful.'

And she says:

'It's all right: nobody's perfect. I still love you.'

The Long Goodbye

Georgie, Lydia's oldest friend, is coming over: her final visit before going off to university. All the others have gone. She's the last.

Lydia isn't going anywhere yet, thank God. That I'm just about managing without Lawrence is partly due to her. With a bit of effort she can annoy me enough for two, and the house certainly looks as if it has several teenagers living in it; with the clothing rail she's put beside her sewing table, the look in the living room is now Sweat Shop Chic, the cold teas left behind at night suggestive of previous workers who've died at their machines and been removed.

They're going to watch the video of their Duke of Edinburgh Silver expedition: fifteen minutes of their team of four trudging along with their huge, fifteen-kilo packs, laughing, singing, accidentally jumping into streams and daring each other to step in cowpats. The denouement is the lid coming off someone's peanut butter in their backpack. Who brings a jar of peanut butter on a twelve-mile hike across wet fields? On the other hand, Shackleton took over two and a half thousand jars of jam to the Antarctic, *and* a load of bottled fruit, so it is in the great British exploring tradition.

It's a world away from anxiety about hair, selfie-ready skin, thigh gaps and what porn has done to the expectations of some of their male peers. When I was their age society was more sexist, but in some ways we were freer, which makes the sight of their carefree faces all the more poignant. Yet their muddy camaraderie leaves me optimistic; I feel their daughters will be off to a good start.

I go upstairs to do a bit of work and when I come back, the two of them are under a blanket on the sofa, watching *Mary Poppins*.

The children loved it when they were small, so I thought I knew every line. Still, not having seen it for a good few years, I'm surprised at how crisp and fresh it still seems. I'm also caught off guard by the emotional impact of the ending, one of the great tearjerkers.

I used to cry only when she leaves; now even the sequence with the fairground horses makes me misty-eyed. I've made the mistake of joining them for the last bit, provoking myself to tears without having at least had the benefit of the jollier stuff early on.

The girls watch, absorbed but dry-eyed, Lydia giving me sideways glances.

'Sorry,' I say.

'I've told you before – you don't have to hide it!'

'Sorry. OK.'

Blub.

Afterwards they say goodbye, and do their routine of a little chant, a hug and a cross between a handshake and a fist bump. When Georgie used to come over regularly after school, it often seemed that they'd added an extra flourish or two, so it got longer and longer. Her mother Maryanne – who had a real job and was much busier than me – would always tell them to hurry up. And I would feel obliged to join in hassling them. But they looked so happy.

And when they do it now, they're back in Year Seven again, and have not yet encountered life's burdens.

Crumple Zone

'The first time I became aware that my father wasn't indestructible was when he cried after my mother died,' says Peter, who was nine at the time.

And I felt the same shaking of the foundations at six, when my aunt killed herself and I saw my father cry. He was lighting the fire, crumpling the newspaper, then he crumpled too, until his head was almost on the grate. He was never fully at peace again.

But surely we *should* be indestructible. I mean, isn't that our job? I still feel so sad for my father, but, given the choice, who wants crumply parents?

Lately Lydia and I haven't been getting on, and I've been crying a lot. I don't know why, except if it's my old depression coming back, after all these years, I can't face it. At times I fear she just hates me.

There's something else, though. I didn't get on very well with my mother once Dad died, over twenty years ago, and now it's happening with my sister as well. Even talking to my friends hasn't helped.

Eventually I confess to Lydia that I feel terrible all the time and am out of ideas.

'Well, *that's* a relief,' she says. 'I thought it was me.'

'No, no!'

I've been trying to hold in my unwelcome emotions, so as not to look melodramatic and weak, and thus failing to diffuse them. So I've ended up inflicting the stress on *her*. And with Lawrence away, the burden is all the greater. At a time when she's making crucial decisions about her future, it's unforgivable. I feel like grabbing everything in her sewing box and stabbing myself with it.

The issue is still hanging over us when he comes back for the holidays and explains, with a self-assurance that is simultaneously comforting and disconcerting, that I need to stop trying to hold everything in quite so much, or pretending to cope, while taking whatever it is out on them.

'I *know*,' I say. 'But I don't want you thinking I *can't* cope.'

Even though at the moment I can't.

'We don't think that,' says Lydia kindly.

'Because the last thing kids need is to see their parents going to pieces.'

I loved my dad, but there were times when he'd hit some crisis and pour his heart out a bit too much, such as when he fell for a beautiful Yugoslavian waitress while he was still married to my stepmother.

A modern child would probably say:

'Eeww! Too Much Information!' and go back to their phone.

Now, I feel I must protect my children not only from drama, which I hate, but also *neediness*.

'We're talking about sharing a bit of emotion or the occasional problem,' says Lawrence. 'Not "going to pieces".'

'Yeah, but you need to feel safe.'

'We do. So you can gradually show your more . . . vulnerable side, as time goes on. In fact, you need to, to help us grow up.'

'What?'

Whoa.

Not only are my assumptions being overturned, which is unsettling enough, but I'm receiving parenting advice from my own kids.

Then, just when I'm thinking: *Ooh they're so wise*, they wander off, leaving their mugs and ice-cream wrappers all over the table and I want to shout at them. So I guess it balances out.

And I do have an ally. If I 'weaken', there's always Peter to step in. But when does sharing becoming *leaning*?

'How do I gradually let down my guard, as it were? When?'

'Now is good,' says Lawrence. 'Now we're older.'

And Lydia agrees.

He is twenty, and next year she will be too.

It's easy to forget that they go on maturing when you're not looking. Since he's been living away, I've sometimes found myself thinking he's at the same point as when we last saw him, as if he's a photograph. We modern parents tend to believe our offspring can't develop without our constant attention. But of course it's the other way round.

When he was about to come home for the first time, I realized he no longer had an Oyster card and texted him:

Hey, u got no Oyster 4 London.

But having sent that, I remembered:

Hang on, u can now use debit card 4 tube etc!

And he texted back:

What a time to be alive.

For a moment I feel as though we're back in Grenada, setting off to go snorkelling, except that Lawrence is the guy in the boat.

'But how will I know when I'm being – you know – human, normal or whatever, or needy and unable to protect you?'

He gets up and reaches for his bass.

'Don't worry, OK? We'll let you know.'

'But—'

He kisses the top of my head. I feel about five.

'Ssh, it's all going to be fine.'

'Oh my God, you know who you sound like . . .?'

But he is pressing my head to his chest and can't hear.

Almost Gone Girl

Lydia has got into art school. And it's on the edge of London, so . . .

'This is great! You can live at home! I mean, well done.'

'No way! You let Lawrence move out.'

'Yes, but he's in Manchester.'

'The facilities are all open till ten every night! I want to be able to work late.'

This is, let's not forget, the child who had to be pulled away from her foil and chicken-wire Pegasus at 10.30, was sent to bed, waited till *we'd* gone to bed, then *got up secretly* and worked on it till 2 a.m.

'It is in Zone 6, though: bit mad not to live here.'

'This is so unfair.'

'I just crave your gorgeous presence with me at all times.'

'So it's nothing to do with the money.'

'Of course it's to do with the money.'

I try to carry on arguing, but my heart's not in it.

'You're right,' I say. 'It would be cruel to tear you away from your drawing board every night – not to mention the great social life you'll be having.'

Since her friends have left, it's been pretty quiet round here.

'So I *will* be moving out?'

'Of course; don't worry.'

'Don't leave me with her!' says Peter.

I can't believe we've reached this point at last.

The Way We Live Now

The world is a different place from when I first got pregnant, twenty-one years ago.

It's January 2018. We're on the plane, coming back from holiday in Tenerife, when the flight attendant asks for our attention.

I feel my hands tighten on the armrests. Lawrence and Lydia immediately pick up the tension and look over.

She says:

'We have a passenger on board with a nut allergy. So we're kindly requesting that if you're travelling with any nuts in your hand luggage, you do not open them while on board.'

In Trafalgar Square, dead white male Admiral Nelson is still on his column, but looking down on pedestrian crossings with green and red LGBT symbols telling you when to cross, where there used to be just single – presumed heterosexual – men.

'Message', 'access' and 'impact' have become trans verbs.

Avocados in multipacks are labelled *Eat Now* and *Eat Later* – don't get them mixed up, now – and chocolate buttons carry a sequence of three pictures that show you how to open the packet, then seal it with a little adhesive square stuck on the side.

We're living through an age of unprecedented good health and opportunity among the educated and affluent, with more and more safety measures, yet we're more anxious than ever.

I blame reading.

When we had Lawrence I was given *The Baby and Toddler Meal Planner* which I never used. Sorry, Mother; fine words puréed no parsnips round these parts. But the one that most demoralized me was the American book *What to Expect*, with its forbidden foods and drinks, and endless *goals*; hey, here's another thing for you to fail at! After a paediatrician diagnosed Lawrence with Developmental Delay at eight months, all the 'experts' except Dr Spock were thrown out.

Then as time went on, these 'authorities' continued to pile in and we were told more and more different – and inevitably conflicting – ways to Get It Right. Solutions that came and went included *Secrets of the Baby Whisperer: All Your Problems Solved* – unlikely, if not impossible; *Attachment Parenting* – wear the baby on you 24/7 till you no longer exist as a separate entity; and *Contented Baby* – Miserable Everyone Else. The number of books available in 2018 is too high to count, but here's one that seems to epitomize the age:

Dailygreatness – yes, it is one word – is 'a practical guide for raising conscious kids . . . a tool for personal and family transformation and the ultimate journal for staying conscious and stress free while recording the amazing experience of being a parent.'

But a lot of the parenting experience is not amazing; it's exhausting, unrewarding and very *boring*. So some of us would actually prefer to be a teeny bit *less* conscious. Plus now, it's a minefield too.

Recently I met a woman who told me two things: one, the list of substances banned from packed lunches at her child's school is now so long – it includes *houmous* – she's given up making them; and two, she saw someone in ultra-smart, privileged Kensington Gardens spray a swing with disinfectant before putting her child on it. 'Nil points for immunology,' as my mother would have put it.

Then on the train I sit opposite a well-dressed young mother whose toddler is drinking out of a smart pink box.

'I like the box,' I say.

'She takes her milk to school in it,' she says.

'Handy.'

'Actually she's on cashew milk.'

'Ah, lactose intolerant?'

And she looks at me blankly.

'Well, it's not confirmed – yet.'

Leaving aside the lack of vital calcium, iodine and vitamins D and B12 in pretend milk, what happens at school when the cashew and almond milk brigade clash with the nut allergists? Given the growing numbers of both factions, I can see it taking off as an alternative sport, like cage fighting for the health and safety age. If the action flags, they could bring in the anti-glutenites. I'd pay to see it.

When I went to that talk on the teenage brain and reconsidered peer pressure, it dawned on me that the people who imitate each other the most are parents.

Take transport. Four-wheel drives, once the preserve of farmers, white Kenyans and the Queen, are now the default: huge vehicles with enough off-road traction to storm the compound of a mid-level Afghan warlord while sipping a huge container of boiling liquid and texting the violin teacher. They're just bigger – not safer, but *feel* as though they are, which is what counts. And of course walking to school has become more risky. Children killed per year by random strangers: between four and five; by vehicles: around fifty.

Buggies have also become obese.

The one Peter found in a skip when Lawrence was a baby was like a wire coat-hanger compared with the current fat-tyred, £1,200 mobile child thrones such as the Bugaboo Buffalo – why not try it in 'Grey Melange' – or the new iCandy All-Terrain, an 'ingenious collaboration with iconic brand Land Rover' for £1,500. You'd no more fold this lot up than you would an actual Land Rover; it'd mean unloading the baby plus all that kit. And anyway, why should you? Baby takes precedence. When a mother and a wheelchair user got into a row on a bus over who was entitled to the space in the middle, it went all the way to the Supreme Court. The wheelchair user won; apparently he really couldn't get out.

And why do we all get those padded bags to hold a few spare nappies, a bottle and some wipes? That have to match the buggy. What's wrong with a normal bag? And why *padded*? In case Mummy goes mad and has to be dragged away, screaming and babbling, swiping at Daddy and anyone else within range? Maybe women will start matching the buggies themselves: 'This charming navy stretch onesie features cute gambolling rabbits, and sleeves that do up at the back . . .' And do we really need a 'changing table'? Basically a sideboard with a baby on top instead of a dressed ham. And don't forget to get a food puréeing machine, which is not at all the same as the blender you already have. Oh no, wait: it is.

Back when we had our two we thought there was a lot of stuff for sale. Among the items my mother thought I'd made up as a joke were a big plastic clip to put over the toilet seat so baby couldn't climb in and drown, baby dungarees with padded inserts so they didn't hurt their knees while crawling, and 'healing beads' made of amber:

'Rash, temperature, photophobia: it could be meningitis!'

'Here: have a yellow necklace.'

Not so long ago we treated real fears with real information; as smoking declined, for example, so did the number of cot deaths.

Now we're starting to resemble a remote, superstitious culture – *Homo Timens* – that puts its problems in the hands of witch doctors who take our money and give us magic beads and potions – and also gadgets. Everyone else is getting them, so they must ward off danger, right?

Our friend Max's baby monitor came with an extra – a sensor to put under the mattress, which vibrated when the baby was 'too still', then sounded an alarm. He said:

'It kept waking the baby with its jiggling, *and* scaring the hell out of us with the alarm. We dumped it after one night.'

As I write this, in May 2018, there are twenty-five video baby monitors on johnlewis.com – and that's not including the purely audio ones. And for twenty-four-hour wraparound worry, there's the Smart Nursery, an 'integrated ecosystem' with 'unrivalled levels of analytics and interoperability'.

If you need to watch your baby *interoperably* while you're at work, have you forgotten to get a nanny?

And if you look away, will you be found less attentive than your peers? Guilty of thinking about something else?

Our friend Angela put her children, born in the eighties, in the garden for naps in their prams.

'Within earshot, though: not down the far end, like my mother's lot used to do.'

As probably the last woman to do it at all, she should have her own waxwork in Madame Tussauds. Her children, now parents themselves, wouldn't dream of doing anything so extreme. I didn't do it either. Yet those of us with the firmest security measures seem to be those who fear the outside world the most. Isn't the idea of getting all this stuff to help us worry *less*?

When not under twenty-four-hour surveillance, *Timens* Junior is at the playground, with its super-safe spongy underlay, being helped on and off the apparatus, and not a grazed knee in sight. Dad's the most attentive, hopping from foot to foot with arms outstretched, like a goalie anticipating a ball that never comes.

'Well done, Arya!' he cheers, as she manages to slide all of a metre unaided, or swing through an angle of four degrees. Next he's clambering about after her on the climbing frame, an invasive species disturbing the ecosystem like a horse in the canopy of the rainforest.

And when she's hungry she won't get *sweets* – oh no – but 100 per cent natural 'fruit paws' – at £2.50 for a hundred grams with 37.8 per cent sugar, the most expensive way to rot your child's teeth since slave-grown monosaccharides became all the go five hundred years ago. And this from people who won't let her have chips.

He and Arya are meeting Mummy and baby Tyrion for supper, which would be fine if they were Spanish or Italian – because *they* play sweetly with a wooden spoon while their twenty-five relatives talk incredibly loudly all around them, then doze off adorably on a cushion.

But they're not Spanish or Italian; they're from London, where, by 7 p.m., they become quite tired:

'AAAAARGH!!'

'What is it, Tyrion? Don't you want your *risotto ai porcini*?'

'AAARGH!'

Bang, Bang, BANG! with the spoon. Concerned Daddy gets up and crouches by the highchair, like *The Adoration of the Magi*.

'Would you like something else instead? Tell Daddy what you'd like.'

More screaming and banging, greeted by bafflement: what on earth could be making a toddler who's been up for fifteen hours so *distressed*?

What to do?

Let's go to the cinema! The children are so intelligent they can follow any storyline, and anyway the babysitter hasn't been born who could match up to their Ming dynasty-grade domestic requirements. The vital bonding process need not be interrupted.

Naturally they are sitting just behind us.

'MUMMY? MUM*MEEEEE*!'

'What is it, darling?'

'WHAT'S THAT MAN DOING?'

'He's telling the lady that if he doesn't make holes in all her sheep to let the air out of their tummies, they'll die.'

'WHY? WHY IS HE DOING THAT? *WHY*?!'

'Because he wants her to marry him instead of the other man. Well, actually two other—'

'I'VE GOT A BIG POO IN MY BOTTOM!'

'All right, darling, just a minute.'

'IT'S COMING OUT – NOW!!'

Whatever happened to Couples' Time?

What's become of the Good Enough Parent?

And what the hell are these people going to do when – *if* – their children ever move out?

Uber has liberated some of us from giving lifts to older kids, with the result that there are now teenagers who've never been on public transport. Some parents think buses are mobile non-secure units for the deranged, and of course they *are*, but that also makes them invaluable training facilities for spotting creeps and weirdos before you encounter them at work. If you ever get that far. The Bugaboo-to-Uber child will never be mugged on the night bus. But will they find it harder to cope with university in a strange town? Maybe in the future they'll go everywhere in special transfer pods, inside tubes like those sealed corridors that take you from the terminal to the plane but without the scary strangers. Actually, since it seems that autonomous vehicles might catch on, that's not so unlikely. We're promised our own individual ones, for maximum personal freedom – and isolation. And less freedom for the young, whose parents will still know where they are at all times.

A group of guests at our kitchen table recall how much more relaxed things were in the past.

'I used to walk to school, when I was about eight. Now, people won't let their kids go *anywhere*.'

'I blame social media: there's too much ability to be in touch all the time.'

'Yes!' says another. 'They track them via their phones.'

These are not our friends but Lawrence's.

'Listen to this,' says a girl possibly named Harry. 'My parents were away, and when they came back – a bit earlier than expected – I was out.'

'How old were you?' I ask.

'Eighteen! I didn't know they were back. After the gig or whatever it was, I went back to a friend's. My phone was off. And they went crazy.'

They started panicking, phoning and texting her friends. At 9 a.m. they rang the police.

'They had the dogs out – everything.'

'They just have too much ability to be in touch,'

says one of the others. 'There's Find My iPhone, Oyster tracking . . .'

Another chips in:

'My friend was tracked by his parents via an app on his phone.'

'Really?'

'If he turned it off, they cut off his allowance.'

'How old was he?'

'Seventeen.'

I never imagined a time when we'd have our own kids under surveillance.

'But *why*?'

She pauses for a moment. 'I think it was to make sure he wasn't buying dope.'

It doesn't do that, though, does it? After all, the pulsing white dot in *Alien* shows us where the monster is; it doesn't save the crew.

Light at the End of the Tunnel

Lawrence is down for the holidays. I'm getting the hang of the routine now. The first bit, when he's just arrived, is not always easy, but the rest is starting to feel more normal, and the delicious meals he makes when he's here definitely help.

He is in the hall, with his bass on his back.

'I'll see you later. I'm just going over to Cameron's.'

'D'you need a lift?'

Despite the statistical unlikelihood of his being mugged for a second-hand left-handed bass, I worry. And it is South London, a transport Bermuda Triangle.

'Nah, it's fine. I'm meeting the others.'

'Others . . .?'

OMG.

He's in a band.

The first band was back in Year Eight. One of us would drive him with his bass over to the house where the drummer lived, because whoever has the drum kit has to host, and Alex, the abnormally well-organized guitarist, would always ring first not only to give him the rehearsal time but to remind him to bring a packed lunch. I bet Jimi Hendrix never had someone to do that for him; his life could have been so different. Anyway, that boy will go far.

The next thing we know, they've lined up a gig.

'Can we come? Can we come? Please please please *please*?'

'Not really.'

It's in Manchester, at a tiny venue, and they're not ready to be seen yet, by us. Or, for all we know, anyone.

The next gig is bigger – but still in Manchester and still too soon for us to come. Actually, it is extremely soon.

I say:

'Do you think you should organize some rehearsals?'

Alert: you are close to your Helicoptering Allowance for this month.

'What, before performing in front of two hundred people? Why would we do that?'

A couple of days later I'm heading downstairs and hear music: music I don't recognize, but rather like. *Mmm, an eclectic sort of style . . . production's a bit rough.* Then I realize it's *live*. They're rehearsing!

I hurriedly text Peter THYRE PLAYG IN TH

KTCHN but he doesn't reply so I dial his number, then press the red button so he can hear them for himself, but I just get a mystified *DID U CALL?* So I surreptitiously try to record them on my phone by propping it up against the coffee jar while pretending to boil the kettle, but fail to secure it properly so it crashes noisily to the floor – just as they all get to the end of the song and look up.

Just behave normally.

'That was so good!'

'Hey, thanks,' they say politely. 'Are you coming to the gig?'

WE'V BN INVITD TO A GIG!

The venue is a pub, in nearby Peckham. A couple of the other parents are there too, and Lawrence's girlfriend. She's another beauty, with dark tumbling curls and a Fifties film star figure, and she reads – books!

Lydia arrives with her friends. I know: I'll be the generous parent and offer to buy them all a drink. It'll make her look good too.

'Thanks! A double Captain Morgan and Coke, please,' they all chant sweetly.

This round's about to cost me over £30!

'Yeah, I got them into that,' says Lydia.

Mm, well done.

I debate briefly whether to get the cheaper stuff or even singles, but I don't want to show her up. And it is so nice to see the delighted expressions on their little faces, just like when it was Easter eggs, or fairy cakes with different coloured icing. It must be years since I last bought a round, so that takes me back – in both senses. But what feels really strange is what happens next.

The moment I step through the doorway into the function room, the decades fall away. I've just left school and joined a small music paper, on £2,800 – a year. I'm eighteen again, only instead of Linx or Incognito onstage it's my child, who's roughly the same age, in a strange but beautiful time loop. The sensation is so vivid, I almost reach for my notebook.

I drift off into my memories.

Then I realize I'm moving.

To the beat.

And so is Peter, just a little.

Oh no . . .

I once nodded my head to a song – *and mouthed some of the lyrics* – at a school concert, and Lydia was so horrified she left the hall. And at the time I thought: *Bit of an overreaction, Drama Queen.* But now I'm cringing retrospectively. If my mother had done that at my school, I would not only have fled the building but run all the way to Dover and got on the next ferry – to anywhere.

I stop dead, and see Lawrence grinning at me.

It's OK! He's not going to jump down off the stage mid-song to march us to the exit. Even so, I keep it to within a square foot or so, to be safe – and because Lydia is not far away, and while he may have come through the Tunnel of Embarrassment into the light beyond, she has not.

After the set we go and sit back down again at the same table, as no one has taken our seats.

'Wow!' I say to Peter. 'This is so great! We can hear *and* we can sit down!'

'Let's quit while we're ahead.'

We say well done to the boys, and I give Lawrence a twenty to get some drinks; being a student he considers this a perfectly decent amount. The sooner we get his sister off to art school, frankly, the better.

So we drift towards the door with an understated wave, but they come over and envelop us in generous hugs.

'Thanks for coming!' they say.

'No, thank *you*!'

We get into the car, and Peter says:

'I feel as though we're in a new phase.'

Though he says this if they put their mugs *and*

their plates in the dishwasher, this time I think he's right.

'When they're little,' he muses, 'you take them for playdates and talk to the other parents and so on. Then when they become teenagers they can't mix you with their friends any more, because they're trying out their new selves and they don't want you to see.'

And because suddenly you've become a hideous liability, unable to perform the most rudimentary social transaction, such as asking, 'Would any of you like something to eat?' without causing them to recoil in horror and hurl themselves screaming from the room.

'And now?'

'Now . . . we're – adults, and so are they, almost. Before, it was a bit like we were some old item of clothing they were forced to wear; they had to keep shaking us off.'

As if we'd suddenly gone out of fashion: *parents – they're just so last year.*

'And now we're on equal ground. They don't feel responsible for our behaviour any more.'

And I no longer tell Lawrence, when we bump into people, to say hello.

'They were quite good, weren't they?'

'Yeah. I'm so glad we never paid for music lessons.'

Considering what we've just spent on double Captain Morgans, it's just as well.

Life Skills

Lydia sits me down at the table.

'Right, Mum. I'm going to show you something.'

'Er – OK.'

She produces a cardboard box from a paper carrier and takes out a piece of fried chicken. It smells lovely.

'OK, pick it up.'

I take it and bring it up to my mouth.

'No, don't eat it. Hold it, like this. And just bite off the end. Now, you see that bit just peeping out there? Take that, and pull.'

It's a bone. I remove it.

'Now, do the same with this . . .'

The second bone also slides out easily. There is just flesh and crispy coating left.

'Ooh.'

She gestures, and I put it in my mouth.

'*Mmm*. That is delicious.'

'And that is How You Eat Wings.'

I guess she feels, now that she's passed this on, that I am ready for her to leave.

And Lawrence? I can officially stop worrying about him, for I now have definitive proof that he is a grown-up. From a launderette in Manchester he texts:

Guy gave me a free wash while he was fixing the machine. Literally the Best Day Ever.

Coda

Peter has taken Lydia to her Halls of Residence and the house is eerily quiet. There are no platforms, fake-fur coats or cans of Venom in the hall; no random damp towels draped over the banisters.

I put on Radio 4 and start the supper. It still feels too quiet.

I know – I'll listen to one of Lawrence's playlists, with the good speakers he convinced me to buy myself for Christmas.

Remember to wait for the Bluetooth . . .

Remember to *select* the speakers, not just gaze blankly at them.

The room fills with music.

Ah, that's better.

I go over to the back door to close the curtains, and see his bass, lying across the sofa. When I lift it, I find it's still plugged into the amp.

Acknowledgements

Once again, I've been the beneficiary of the commercial and creative brilliance of the best agent in the world, Mark Lucas. Both he and my editor, George Morley, inspired and cajoled me to produce work infinitely better than I could have managed alone. I'd also like to thank the copy-editor Jessica Cuthbert-Smith, Laura Carr, Liz Marvin and Chloe May, whose efforts smoothed away those remaining flaws that could be smoothed.

My husband and fellow writer Peter Grimsdale urged me not to pull my punches, as well as being endlessly willing to have his carelessly uttered words recorded and exposed on the page for the benefit and entertainment of others.

To Lawrence and Lydia, who were so generous with the material from their own lives and tolerated my interpretation of it, I am also deeply indebted. And thanks go to Lawrence's friends for sharing their acute and invaluable observations on the age of surveillance.

Sophie Doyle is owed huge thanks for courage in the face of receipts, lists, sudden texts and piles of family archive blocking the way to the desk. She makes our lives less chaotic and is indispensable. I'm also indebted to the wonderful people on the 10th floor of North Wing.

Thanks go also to all those dear friends who gamely allowed me to include their own experiences and mishaps: Patrick Tatham, Karen Stirgwolt, Lucy Lindsay, Jon Price, Jo Hage, Sarah Beardsall, Sarah Harding, Diane McDonald, Angela Neuberger, Max Neuberger, James Castle, Liz and Gabriel Irwin, Susie and Justin Foulds, Alan Bookbinder, Jessica Ray, Jane Gaspar, Tilly Vosburgh and Teresa Howard. Teresa's advice on page 222 is worth the cover price.

I'm also grateful to my sister, the novelist Claire Calman, for her morale-boosting emails and forensic standards of fact checking, for example of the exact workings of Katie Kopycat.

My mother, Pat McNeill, who died while I was writing this book, was a sceptic who showed by her example how to resist the fads and commercially driven scaremongering which have increasingly colonized the field of parenting. My writing has benefitted hugely from her influence.

Finally, a huge and heartfelt thank you to Katarina

Petruscakova, who's evolved over twenty years from nanny and domestic troubleshooter to friend and irreplaceable member of the family. That our offspring are in such good shape is due in no small part to her invaluable contribution.